Tight
Lines,
Bright
Water

Tight Lines, Bright Water

Travels with a Fly Fisherman

Dave Engerbretson

Solstice Press
Moscow, Idaho

DEDICATION

This book is dedicated to:
My parents who instilled in me the love of the outdoors.
Tom Krizan, the man who first taught me to cast a fly;
George Harvey, the man who put it all together;
Jeff, Eric and Shirley, my fishing partners.

A Solstice Press book produced at North Country Book
Express, Inc., by Melissa Rockwood, Karla Fromm, Mary
Schierman and Jennifer Brathovde under the direction of
Patricia Hart and Ivar Nelson.

Designed by Melissa Rockwood
Cover illustration by Emily Silver
Photographs by Dave Engerbretson
Photos printed by Joe Dvorak

ISBN: 0-932722-13-X
10 9 8 7 6 5 4 3 2 1

Contents

Acknowledgements

A book of this type would be impossible without the help and encouragement of a great many individuals. I would like to offer my sincere thanks and appreciation to Patricia Hart and Ivar Nelson of Solstice Press for suggesting the work, convincing me to do it, and for their editorial assistance. Thanks, too, to the great staff at Solstice who helped it all come together, Karla Fromm, Mary Schierman, Jennifer Brathovde, Opal Gerwig, Patty McCauley, Rob Moore, and Melissa Rockwood; to Emily Silver for her cover art; to Joe Dvorak for his outstanding work in the darkroom; and to all of the editors who have given me support with my work during my years as a writer.

A very special and loving thanks to my wife, Shirley, and stepdaughter, Jenny, who spent many long hours transposing old manuscripts to computer disks. This book truly would have been impossible without their willing help, love and constant support.

D.L.E.

Preface

I've never really understood why men and women put so much time and effort, money and emotion into catching a small fish that most often is released again anyway. I know that my own investment in this pursuit is not as great as for some, but is considerably more than that of many others. But why?

It would take a better philosopher than I to answer such a mystical question, but I do know that I must be one of the luckiest men alive. I love fly fishing, and I often get paid to do it, to write about it, to photograph it and to talk about it. Such a job is a dream come true.

So this book will not try to answer the question of *why* people go fishing, or even why I go fishing. It will tell you *how* I became a fly fisherman, and it will share with you some of the adventures that I've had and a few of the tricks that I've learned along the way. Some of the chapters have been published before as magazine articles, some have been revised from old articles and some are new. I hope that all of them will be enjoyable reading, will give you the necessary information to allow you to repeat the adventures for yourself, and will increase your enjoyment of the wonderful world of fly fishing.

Since some of these chapters were originally written as magazine articles over a period of years, I hadn't realized until they were assembled into the complete book manuscript how many times I had used the term "paradise" in reference to many of the locations about which I have written. I suppose this isn't really too surprising, since I have been very fortunate to have had the opportunity to cast my flies into some of the best waters the world has to offer, and I want to share those experiences with you here. Thus, I have left the references to "paradise" in the manuscript, as the pieces were originally written.

So — sit back and relax, and let's go fly fishing together.

May you have many tight lines and bright waters.

D.L.E.
Moscow, Idaho
July, 1986

The Making of a Fly Fisherman

I don't know why people become fly fishers. I suppose there are as many reasons as there are anglers, but I've thought about the matter a great deal. More precisely, I've thought about why I became a fly fisher, but I don't know that either.

To say that someone was 'born to be an artist,' 'born to be a lawyer,' or 'born to be' anything at all doesn't answer the question and is certainly a well worn cliché. But in my case, I can't think of any other explanation—I guess I was born to be a fly fisherman.

I don't know how else to account for the fact a ten-year-old boy living in the farming country of southern Minnesota, and who had never seen anyone even cast a fly *knew* that someday he would be a fly fisherman. But I did. I can't recall if I saw it in the movies, or *Field & Stream*, or what turned me on, but I knew that someday I would do it.

My family had a small cabin on Lake Shetek, a large, warm water lake that held only bullheads, crappie, walleye, northern pike and carp, and no one in the area fished with flies. Someone had given my dad an old South Bend fly rod, though, and he found it to be just the ticket for fishing crappies off the dock—with a bait casting reel, braided casting line, a bobber, sinker, and minnows.

As soon as Dad would leave for work, I'd take the fly rod from its nails on the cabin wall, cut off the heavy terminal tackle and try to cast like they did with flies. I just could not make it work as I knew it should. I couldn't figure out how they did it, and it drove me nearly crazy trying to figure it out. If only someone would have told me that you needed a special fly line!

I don't know what was inside of me that drove me to want to fly fish, but the feeling wouldn't go away despite my inability to cast with Dad's crappie rod. I'd try to cast, become frustrated and quit, and then a week or so later, I'd try again. I had to be doing something wrong, but what?

This sorry state of affairs continued for several years, and though I had almost given up trying to cast Dad's rod, the thought of someday being a fly fisherman never left my mind. Yet I have no idea just why the feeling remained so strong.

One day, while walking down Main Street in my home town of Tracy, Minnesota, I stopped in my tracks. There, in the window of Rignell's hardware store was a fly rod! The price tag said eight dollars. Of course, I didn't have eight dollars, but I knew that somehow that rod would be mine.

I don't recall how long it took me to earn the money for that rod, or how I managed to do it, but I do remember that every time I walked by Rignell's I held my breath until I made sure that no one else had bought "my" fly rod. There was little danger of that, though. Fly rods were not high priority items in Tracy.

I'm sure that my parents thought that I had taken complete leave of my senses the day that I proudly walked into the house with my new fly rod. "What in the world are you going to do with that?" they asked.

"Fish," I replied, and they both simply shook their heads. Of course, I still didn't know that you needed a special reel and fly line. But, no matter. I had my first fly rod.

As special as my new rod was, I cannot recall what I did with it, or what happened to it. But I can still shut my eyes and remember exactly how it felt — whippy, slow, and very tip heavy. The True Temper Telescoping Steel Fly Rod was not a delicate instrument. I thought it was wonderful.

My preoccupation with fly fishing did not cause me to neglect the rest of my fishing education, however. Spending my summers on Lake Shetek allowed me to fish whenever I felt like it, and I felt like it about every day. My front yard was the lake, and I was as at home in and on the water, as any other kid would have been in his front yard. I fished with a cane pole and worms for bullheads, or with "minnies" for crappies. Or I'd fish with casting gear for walleye and northern pike. I just plain liked to fish.

Every angler has a wealth of stories of the "big one that got away," and I started my collection at an early age. The first time that it happened is as fresh in my mind as if it had happened yesterday. I had taken my casting rod and a Daredevel down to the lagoon at Teepeeota Point to cast for northerns, and after casting without success for a half hour or so something smashed my lure with a vengeance. The water exploded and the reel handle was jerked from my grip as the biggest fish that I'd ever hooked headed for open water.

Knowing nothing of how to play a big fish, I figured the harder he pulled the harder I had to pull, so I did. The line parted with a loud snap! — and my response was instantaneous. I flung the rod to the sand and leaped into the lake. Standing there in water almost to my neck, I said out loud, "Why did I do that?"

No one is quite as embarrassed as a young teenager who knows that he's done something really stupid.

In junior high school and high school I played all of the usual team sports, and since it was a small school, many of the athletes also played in the band. Our band director, Jerry Rood, had a summer cabin in

northern Minnesota, and I knew that he was a fisherman, but I couldn't believe it when someone told me that he fished for trout with flies.

One day after junior high band practice I walked into Mr. Rood's office, and said, "I understand that you fish with flies?" He replied that he did, and I blurted out, "Well, how do you do it?"

"Oh, the usual way," he answered. "Dry flies upstream and wet flies downstream."

And I knew that I'd asked another dumb question. We never talked of fly fishing again, but from that moment on I had a new respect for Mr. Rood. After all, he was a fly fisherman.

My desire to fish with flies smoldered through my college years, and fanned to full flame again when I accepted my first teaching position in 1958 in the high school at Two Harbors, Minnesota, on the shore of Lake Superior. Trout country!

I was single, and living in a small cabin on the edge of town, and I had lots of free time after school and on weekends to fish, hunt, and explore the woods. Naturally, my thoughts were on trying to catch trout with flies. I didn't know anyone who was a fly fisherman, but the local hardware store sold me some trout flies, and a small, clear plastic bubble that would allow me to cast them with my Zebco spincasting outfit.

The store owner gave me directions to what he assured me was a fine trout stream, and I found the river and rigged my tackle for my first trout fishing expedition. You'd better believe that I was excited. Disappointment quickly overcame the excitement, though, when I stepped into the stream. It was only about twenty feet wide, and hardly more that knee deep. The water was a series of small pools and riffles, and was sparkling clear.

Now I know that it was a perfect little trout stream, but at the time it seemed so shallow, and I sure couldn't see any fish. So I walked directly up the middle of the stream in search of deep water where there should be some trout. I didn't find any, and as I recall, I didn't even wet a fly.

Eventually, though, I learned more about trout fishing, and began to catch a few with my trusty Mepps spinner, and even a few small brook trout on flies ahead of the little plastic bubble. But I knew that I wasn't really fly fishing.

One day, while fishing for brookies, I was standing on a beaver dam and casting into its pool on the Knife River when a huge fish engulfed my little Mepps spinner and tore off across the pool. The monster tried to dive under a brush pile, but he was no match for my heavy spinning line. I finally beached the fish and stared at it in wonder. I had never seen anything like it, and I had no idea what it was. I knew that it wasn't a rainbow or a brook trout, and it wasn't a sucker or whitefish or carp. But what was it?

It was golden brown with black and red spots and was kind of pretty. It must be a good fish whatever it was. Naturally, I killed it, and took it home to show my friends and try to find out if it was good to eat.

When I arrived home, I spotted a neighbor working in his garage, so I walked over and laid the fish out on the floor. "What in the world is this?" I asked.

"That, my friend, is a German brown trout," he said as his eyes widened.

The fish weighed just over six pounds, and to this day I have never caught a bigger brown trout.

A move to St. Paul in 1959 took me away from trout country, but not from thoughts of fly fishing. During a short stay in the hospital, I found myself with time on my hands, and my wife brought me a little Hank Roberts fly tying kit to occupy my time. I read through the small manual and tied my first fly while sitting in a hospital bed.

I wish that I'd have saved that fly — it was an abomination. The size 10 Black Gnat had a scraggly tail, and hackle splayed in every direction. The chenille body was so fat that it almost closed the gap of the hook, but it didn't matter for I couldn't have tied the fly to a leader anyhow. The eye was completely closed by the large, bulky thread head. And so I became a fly tyer, but I still didn't know how to fish with flies.

My chance to be a real fly fisherman finally came in 1960 when I moved to Urbana, Illinois to become a graduate student at the University of Illinois. While looking through the college catalog, I discovered that the Physical Education Department offered a class in fishing, and it was taught by someone named Tom Krizan. Since I was to be a student in that department, it was an easy matter to meet Tom Krizan.

Tom explained to me that students in his class had the opportunity to learn either bait casting, spin casting, or fly casting, and that I would be welcome to sit in on the class if I wanted to do so. He would also lend me a fly fishing outfit to use. I thought about it for maybe three milliseconds, and signed up.

The first day of class, Tom demonstrated the basics of fly casting and what we would be learning during the semester, but we didn't have the chance to try it. I don't remember what other classes I was taking that semester, or how much I studied them, but I practiced fly casting during every spare minute that I had. I would cast on the front lawn between classes and after dinner, and when it got dark I would cast under the street light. By the time the next fishing class met, I could do everything Tom had demonstrated the first day.

Every day I learned something new in class, and I would spend hours practicing casting on my lawn between class meetings. Eventually I scraped together enough money to buy my own outfit — an Eagle Claw "Sweetheart" fiberglass rod, and a three dollar Pflueger Progress reel. Tom gave me a fly line.

One day Tom announced to the class that we should all try to get down to the local sporting goods store that Saturday to see Johnny Dikeman who would be in town to put on a demonstration. I didn't know who Dikeman was, but Tom explained that he was the current World Champion caster.

That Saturday, I'm afraid that I made a pest of myself with Johnny Dikeman. I spent the entire day watching every show he did and plying him with questions in between. I watched him teach others, and I received help with my own casting. I suspect that Dikeman was happy to see the day end, but I learned a great deal about casting a fly.

Tom and his wife, Lois, owned a cabin on a reclaimed strip mine near town, and they had stocked their ponds with bass and panfish. The ponds were a perfect training ground for a novice fly fisherman, and I spent two years honing my newfound skills on bass, sunfish and bluegills.

While at Illinois, Tom helped me to join the American Casting Association (ACA), and to become certified as a casting instructor in bait, spin and fly casting. As a graduation present, Tom took me to Chicago and entered me in the first National Indoor Casting Tournament sponsored by the ACA. I didn't place in the tournament, but I learned a little more about fly casting.

My first opportunity to catch trout came following my graduation from the University of Illinois when I accepted a position at Northeastern University in Boston in 1962. The fact that New England represented the epitome of eastern trout fishing to me, had absolutely nothing to do with my accepting the position — well, maybe just a little bit to do with it.

I spent three years in New England, and every summer I worked as a backpacking guide in New Hampshire, Vermont and Maine. I spent hundreds of hours tramping through the mountains with a fly rod strapped to my pack, and I learned a little more about trout fishing. I still didn't know another fly fisherman, but I practically memorized every word of Ray Bergman's *Trout*.

I came to realize that if I was going to make a career of teaching in universities, that I would need another degree, so in 1965 I enrolled in the graduate school at Penn State. I was drawn to Penn State by a new program in exercise physiology under the direction of an internationally known scholar, Dr. Elsworth Buskirk. I knew nothing of limestone spring creeks — but I was to learn.

My first day on campus Dean Ben Massey offered to give me a tour of the college facilities, and as we walked out of his office we saw a professor strolling down the hall toward us. I'm sure the dean had no idea of the significance of the moment when he said, "Dave, I'd like you to meet George Harvey."

George Harvey! I had long known of George's reputation as one of the country's top fly fishermen, and when I discovered that I would be attending Penn State, I planned to try to meet him somehow. But, this was good fortune, indeed.

We didn't have time to say more than, "Nice to meet you," and the usual pleasantries before the dean took me off on the rest of his tour. But at my first opportunity, I returned to George's office to talk fishing. I told George that I really liked to fly fish, and I wondered if he could give me some information on where to go, since I was new to the area. George was pleasant and polite, and he told me about a couple of local streams. I had apparently interrupted him in the middle of a project, though, and he didn't seem inclined to chat, so I thanked him and left. It was a start.

Later I found out that George taught a physical education class in fly tying and that graduate students were welcome to enroll. Naturally I signed up immediately. Prior to that time I had tied flies for about six years, but had never seen another fly tyer. My flies were terrible, and I had made every mistake that it was possible to make. Once George took me in hand, my tying improved dramatically. Finally I could see what to do and how to do it. Finally I was a fly tyer!

George must have seen that I was serious about becoming a fly fisherman, and we hit it off immediately. I never seemed to run out of questions, and George always had answers for me. I'd pester him in his office or call him at home on the phone, and he never turned me away. The first time he invited me to the fly tying room in his home, it was like a trip to Mecca! What an honor!

To shorten a long story, George and I became very close friends. He was my mentor, my fishing partner and my hero. Through George I learned to fish the limestone spring creeks and tie the most delicate of flies. I learned about such things as terrestrials and Tricos, and I learned a philosophy of fly fishing. Thanks to George Harvey, I became a fly fisherman.

During my last three years at Penn State I helped to support myself and my family by tying flies for Orvis, and by selling fishing tackle from my home. Following my graduation, I had the urge to try my hand at writing, and in 1972 my first article was sold to *TRUE* magazine. My first article was sold to *Fly Fisherman* the same year. The rest, as they say, is history.

No, I don't know why I had the burning desire to become a fly fisherman, but I'm glad that I did. My involvement with fly fishing has given me peace and solitude in a hectic world. It has taken me to spectacular places that I otherwise never would have seen, and it has shown me the beauty and wonder of God's creation. Best of all, fly fishing has given me friends around the world whom I never would have known without it.

2.

Idaho Treasures

There are those who remember the "good old days" with sadness: "It's not like it used to be," they lament. "Why, I can remember when a man could fish all day and not see another fisherman. Can't do that today! Shoot! It's gotten to where you almost have to take a number and get into line to fish the ol' Neverkill today."

Others, who had the misfortune to be born too late, have never seen such days and can only wonder, "What was it like, to have a whole stream all to yourself?"

Somehow, fly fishing and solitude seem made for each other. In fact, fly fishing is solitude. No matter how crowded the stream, in the angler's mind there is only the water, the fly and the fish. In the depths of his concentration, the angler finds solitude. But it's usually a fragile thing, easily shattered by the curse of a downstream fisherman, or even a chance glance in his direction.

Thus, most of us only find the illusion of solitude. We embrace it briefly, enjoy it while we hold it, and feel sadness at its passing.

True solitude is another matter. It is real. It has substance. True solitude is not easily broken, but can be turned this way and that in the mind as well as the eye. It can be savored. True solitude, as rare as a fine jewel, is meant to be treasured.

Rare jewels are not easily discovered, but they do exist for those who search for them with care. And for the angler seeking the treasure of solitude, it can be found in the aptly named "Gem State"—Idaho.

When pressed to name a few of Idaho's trout streams, the average angler would likely reply, "Well, the Henry's Fork is one." He might think a bit and add the Snake to his list, and, if his knowledge of geography was something above average, he might, after some pondering, come up with the Salmon River. After that, it is most probable that the list would come to an abrupt end.

Perhaps that's not so strange, though, for a state that many have difficulty even finding on a map. Idahoans are used to being confused with Iowa and Ohio, or to being from "somewhere way out West." In fact, we kind of like it that way—it helps to preserve the solitude on our favorite trout streams.

It was just such anonymity that enabled me to enjoy one of my very best days of fishing. I turned my car south off State Highway 12, the

Lolo Highway, and followed the gravel road into the Nez Perce National Forest of northern Idaho. For eighteen miles the road closely parallels the pristine Selway River, and the driving is difficult because it's all but impossible to keep your eyes off the tumbling water and the magnificent canyon. Deep, quiet pools beckon at every bend, and each dancing riffle calls out for a drifting nymph.

It was the height of the tourist season, but I saw no other anglers that bright, blue August day. Somehow, I resisted the temptation to stop until I reached the campground at the end of the road near the Selway Falls. I signed into the book at the ranger station, donned my fishing gear, and walked alone up the footpath beyond the road's end. The solitude was instant, and it was real.

I walked on until I could no longer stand to look at the sparkling water without fishing it. Even through my waders, the water was icy as I stepped into it, but the shiver that went through my body was most likely from pure excitement. Solitude does that to me.

Born high in the snowfields of the Bitterroot Mountains, the Selway, above the falls, is open to catch-and-release fishing with barbless flies and single hooked lures only, and it is home to the lovely little West Slope cutthroat trout.

My flies floated on water so clear that they seemed to be suspended in air, and bright, deep bodied fish in the twelve- to fifteen-inch range struck at them with abandon. I fished for hours, and the only other humans I saw were a couple of kayakers who waved a greeting as they passed, and a string of riders and packhorses who paraded silently by on the trail high above me. There were no other anglers. It was a day from which dreams are made.

In Idaho, such idyllic days are the rule rather than the exception. That might be difficult to comprehend if you've never visited the state, or if your only experience there has been standing shoulder to shoulder with a horde of other anglers on the Henry's Fork in June. But, then, the entire state of Idaho is hard to comprehend.

With an area of almost 83,000 square miles, Idaho could easily contain the entire states of Maine, New Hampshire, Vermont, Massachusetts, Connecticut, Rhode Island, and about half of New York. Around this vast area, much of it rugged wilderness, are scattered barely over a million people, fewer than are found in almost any major city of the country.

And there is no lack of fishing water. Over 16,000 miles of streams and rivers flow through Idaho, with 945 miles of them having special regulations to insure quality angling. To this can be added 35,375 acres of lakes ranging in size from the huge Pend Orielle — so large and deep that the U.S. Navy has a submarine research station there, to tiny mountain ponds that can only be reached by foot or horseback. Not surprisingly, a wide variety of fish can be found in the state's abundant waters. Smallmouth and largemouth bass and an assortment of panfish inhabit many of the lowland lakes and streams, and rainbow, brown,

Fly fishing in the North Idaho wilderness on Kelly Creek.

brook, Dolly Varden and cutthroat trout, salmon and steelhead are readily available to the cold water angler.

There are many ways to experience the wealth of fishing that is available in Idaho, and all of them are true adventures in every sense of the word. Wilderness outfitters provide guided raft trips on several of the most remote rivers such as the Middle Fork of the Salmon and the main Salmon, and these trips offer excellent fishing for the beautiful West Slope cutthroat trout amidst the state's most magnificent scenery. Other outfitters offer horsepack trips into the backcountry for trout, or jet boat trips into Hell's Canyon — the country's deepest gorge — for some of the best smallmouth bass fishing found anywhere. Hundreds of miles of hiking trails follow the wilderness streams or lead to the high lakes, and logging roads and state highways provide access to the less hearty.

Though there is only one major north–south highway in the state, Highway 95 along its western border, and a couple of east–west highways at either end of it, anglers who wish to do their exploring by car will have little difficulty finding pristine water and beautiful scenery. Close inspection of a state highway map will reveal many improved roads leading into the back country, and fishing is generally available from most of them.

Adventurous anglers with a week or so to spare would do well to simply go "prospecting" with a map, ask some questions in local service stations and sporting goods stores, and search for their own places of solitude. They are there for the finding, and the discovery of your own special place is at least half of the fun. Primitive campsites are readily available throughout the state, and the angler with a tent or camping trailer is sure to find good fishing, beautiful scenery and rare adventure.

Several streams that are easily accessible, but at the same time are wild and uncrowded, are found in the northern part of the state. Prime examples are the Lochsa and the Selway. Forming the boundary between the Clearwater National Forest to the north and the Selway–Bitterroot Wilderness Area to the south, the Lochsa follows close beside a portion of Highway 12, which runs between Missoula, Montana, and Lewiston, Idaho.

First seen by white men on the Lewis and Clark expedition of 1805, this remote wilderness canyon and its river were little known to the casual traveler until as recently as 1962 when Highway 12 — the Lolo Highway — was completed. Despite the highway, the character of the wilderness remains much as it was in the days of Lewis and Clark. Scarred by large, uncontrolled forest fires which burned through the area between 1910 and 1934, the area has been reclaimed by the forests, but huge blackened stumps still stand in silent testimony to the infernos that once raged through the canyon.

While the fishing for native cutthroat, rainbow and Dolly Varden trout can be good anywhere along the Lochsa, the best area is the catch-and-release stretch upstream from the Wilderness Gateway Campground near mile marker 123. Since the instigation of the catch-and-release requirement several years ago, this section of the river has become a prime example of the effectiveness of special regulations in the improvement of fishing quality.

In the Salish Indian dialect, the word "Lochsa" means "rough water," and the river is aptly named. Filled with large boulders, the river tumbles through its narrow canyon in a never ending series of riffles, runs and pools that provide unlimited fishing opportunities for the passing angler. Roadside pull-outs are frequent and allow the angler to simply drive along the stream and stop to fish wherever a pool looks particularly inviting.

My usual technique is to rig two rods — one with a fast sinking tip line and a deep sparkle caddis pupa or other buggy looking nymph, and the other with a floating line, nine or ten foot leader, and a Stimulator, Elk Hair Caddis, or Royal Wulff dry fly. Thus, by driving while wearing my fishing vest, I can get out of the car and fish with either technique. Waders are generally not needed on the Lochsa, since it is an easy matter to scramble along the rocky bank beside the road and fish very effectively. On the other hand, if waders are worn and a suitable crossing can be found, it is possible to hike along the opposite side of the river and fish spots that rarely see a fly, since most roadside anglers never cross the stream. Fish twelve- to fourteen-inches long are common, and some sixteen to eight inches can be expected.

About twenty-six miles downstream from the beginning of the special regulation water, the Lochsa joins the Selway near the town of Lowell, Idaho, to become the Middle Fork of the Clearwater River. An improved gravel road follows the Selway upstream into the Selway–Bitterroot Wilderness Area for eighteen miles before ending at the Selway Falls Campground. Catch-and-release regulations are in effect upstream from the campground, and, while the road ends, a footpath follows close along the river to provide access for fishermen.

The Three Rivers Resort near the confluence of the rivers offers very good accommodations, or anglers can camp in one of the many primitive camping areas along either the Lochsa or the Selway. Most of the areas will have pit toilets and drinking water available, or the self-contained camper can find numerous hideaway spots to simply pull off the road to camp. And that's really the ideal way to experience the true feel of this wilderness area.

Travelers should be warned that virtually no highway services exist between Missoula, Montana, and Lowell, Idaho, and they should, therefore, be prepared with a full tank of gas before leaving Missoula. Fuel and supplies are available in Lowell and west.

Farther to the north, the Coeur d'Alene lake chain offers excellent springtime bass fishing from a canoe or float tube, and the cool, clear waters of the St. Joe National Forest provide opportunities for the trout fisherman seeking wild fish in a remote setting. The best bet for visiting anglers is the St. Joe River which flows in a generally westerly direction between the settlement of Red Ives and St. Maries, a distance of about ninety miles. Again, an improved gravel road follows the river closely, and campsites are available every few miles. Access to the road is either from St. Maries to the west, or by driving thirty miles south off Interstate 90 at Wallace, Idaho.

Fly fishermen will likely find the best fishing on the upper reaches of the St. Joe between the village of Avery, forty-seven miles upstream from St. Maries, and the road's end at Red Ives, thirty-nine miles above Avery. Except for fuel and some groceries at Avery, there are no services after leaving either St. Maries or Wallace.

Above its confluence with Prospector Creek, thirteen miles upstream from Avery, the St. Joe is designated as "Wild Trout Water," and fishing is restricted to barbless flies and single hooked artificial lures only. Three trout in excess of thirteen inches may be kept. Although similar in character to the Lochsa, the upper St. Joe is even more pristine due to the absence of a major highway along its banks.

As in most of Idaho's remote waters, fly patterns are not usually critical, and any high riding dry fly or fast sinking nymph will produce well. It should be noted, though, that the most popular dry fly in Idaho is the Renegade — a simple fore-and-aft style pattern, that, because of its effectiveness, has practically become the "state fly." It is tied with a stiff brown hackle at the rear of the hook shank, a peacock herl body, and a white hackle at the front of the hook. It's dynamite on cutthroat in sizes 10-16.

Of all the remote trout streams in Idaho, my favorites have got to be Kelly Creek and its tributary, Cayuse Creek, deep in the heart of the Clearwater National Forest. Unequaled for mountain scenery, this area provides a wilderness fishing experience at its very best.

There is no easy way to the Kelly Creek area. The gravel roads are long, rough and dusty, and it's far from even the smallest village, but therein lies much of its charm. Mountains rise steeply from the river's edge, the air sparkles with unpolluted clarity, and the water rushes cold and clear. Surely the country has changed little from the days before the white man. When your tent is pitched, and your fire crackles in the dying light of day, you are no longer in the twentieth century.

Kelly Creek can be reached by either of two routes. From the north, turn south off Interstate 90 at Superior, Montana, and follow the "improved" gravel road for about forty miles to the Kelly Creek Ranger Station. From the south, follow State Highway 11 from its intersection with U.S. Highway 12 near Orofino, Idaho, to the village of Pierce, and then continue for about fifty miles on the gravel road to the Kelly Creek Ranger Station. If your car is equipped with a CB radio, it is a good idea to turn it to the channel indicated on the roadside signs to help keep track of the logging trucks that frequent the road. No services of any kind are available after leaving either Pierce or Superior, so plan to fill with gas at those locations.

The Kelly Creek Ranger Station is located at the confluence of Kelly Creek with the North Fork of the Clearwater River, and there is a large campground at the junction of the rivers. From the campground, a rough gravel road runs upstream along Kelly Creek for approximately eleven miles, and fine fishing can be had right from the road. An alternative is to follow the road upstream until it crosses the river, park at the bridge, and fish upstream from there.

From the bridge, a hiking and horsepack trail follows the river, at times swinging high above the water and occasionally dipping down to stream level. Backpacking anglers can follow the trail, make camp along the river, and enjoy superb angling. If you don't wish to backpack, camp can be set up down a little dirt road that turns right just past the bridge. Campers should plan on bringing their own water or boiling river water for drinking. Drinking water is available at the Kelly Creek Ranger Station Campground.

In addition to Kelly Creek, its tributary, Cayuse Creek, can provide excellent fly fishing for those who seek a little variety in the scenery and fishing. To reach Cayuse Creek, follow the gravel road across the Kelly Creek bridge, and continue driving about seven to ten miles up the pass until you come to the Cayuse Creek bridge. The fishing can be very good in either direction from the bridge.

Due to its elevation and normally heavy snowpack, it is often impossible to get into the area until late June, and the fishing is not generally good until well into July. Even better are the months of August and September — grasshopper time when your favorite 'hopper pattern is sure to bring results.

If the 'hoppers aren't on, the Elk Hair Caddis, Stimulator, Royal Wulff, or the good old Renegade are usually effective on top, or the Sparkle Caddis Pupa, G.R. Hare's Ear, or Casual Dress Nymph fished wet. Since the streams are not deep, even the wets can be fished on a dry line with a nine to ten foot leader.

During the 1960s, the population of West Slope cutthroat trout had almost disappeared from the Kelly Creek drainage. In an attempt to preserve the species, a research program was begun, and in 1970 the fishing regulations were changed to permit only catch-and-release fishing with barbless flies and single hooked artificial lures. Since the instigation of the special regulations, these native fish have made a tremendous comeback, and the project now stands as another outstanding model of the effectiveness of catch-and-release management. Fish in the twelve to sixteen inch range can be expected, and some will run considerably larger.

The Lochsa, Selway, St. Joe, Kelly and Cayuse are but a small sample of the fishing to be found in Idaho. Wherever you happen to be in this magnificent and wild state, good fishing is not far away. Those who believe that the angling map of the United States ends at the western border of Montana don't know what they're missing. If it's solitude, scenery and adventure you're after, you would do well to grab a map, pack your camping gear and go exploring. It's all waiting up almost any backroad in Idaho.

3.

The Frying Pan:
The Perfect Trout Stream

Jim Belsey, my son, Jeff, and I sat on the grassy bank of the Frying Pan River and watched Bill Fitzsimmons stalk a very large, very spooky brown trout. The big fish was lying in tight against the bank, and was quietly sipping the colorful green drakes that swirled into the eddy at the head of the little backwater pool.

The scene we viewed was completed by bright green willows lining the stream banks in front of dark red sandstone cliffs that soared above us into the deep blue cloudless sky.

As Bill sent another cast on its way toward the feeding fish, Jim said, "You know, if a person set out to design the perfect trout stream, it would just have to end up looking like the Frying Pan."

I had to agree. The little river is a very comfortable size to fish and it has all the riffles, runs and pools that you'd expect in a prime trout stream. It has an abundance of rainbows, cutthroat, browns and brookies including some real "lunkers." It has a rich insect population, and it flows through a beautiful Colorado mountain canyon. The Pan is easily accessible from the road, and best of all, it offers dry fly fishing during every month of the year! What more could you ask?

Though I had never seen the Frying Pan before, I had thought about it for more than twenty years — ever since I had first read of it in Schwiebert's *Matching the Hatch* as a neophyte fly fisher living in the East. Somehow the Pan had been indelibly stamped into my mind. Maybe it was it's name, or maybe Schwiebert's glowing prose in describing it. Or maybe it was the fact that it was "out West in the Colorado Rockies." But for some reason, in my mind, the Frying Pan seemed to symbolize what trout fishing was all about, and when I finally fished it, I wasn't disappointed.

In contrast to many of the well known western rivers, the Pan is a small, friendly little stream — except for the scenery, it would be right at home anywhere in the East. Only fourteen miles long, it pours out of Reudi Dam above Basalt, Colorado, flows through a narrow canyon and dumps into the Roaring Fork at Basalt. A blacktop road parallels the stream, but, thanks to the thick willows along its banks, many of its stretches offer unexpected solitude.

Despite its modest size, the Frying Pan is a giant with respect to the impact it has had on fly fishing in Colorado, for it was the Pan that served as a research project and provided the initial stimulus for the development of special regulations and the "Gold Medal Waters" designation on the state's prime trout rivers.

Following a rather stormy public meeting in Aspen in 1978, the Colorado Division of Wildlife Commissioners, at the urging of fisheries biologist, Barry Nearing, decided to set aside a limited section of a trout stream to study the effects of catch-and-release fishing. Due to its short length, steady flow and easy accessibility, the Frying Pan was selected for the project.

For the purposes of the study, the two miles of the Pan immediately below Reudi Dam were set aside for catch-and-release fishing only, while the remainder of the river had an eight fish bag limit, bait fishing was permitted and there were no terminal tackle regulations. At the same time, the State stopped stocking catchable size trout in the entire river.

Over the next three years, the impact of the new regulations was remarkable. The success rate in the catch-and-release water quadrupled to 1.2 fish per man hour, while that in the open regulation water dropped to between 0.1 and 0.2 fish per man hour. At the same time, electrofishing indicated that there were very few large fish remaining in the open water — they had been removed by anglers.

Anglers in the open water rarely took a fish larger than twelve inches in length, while in the catch-and-release water trout in the sixteen to twenty inch class were fairly plentiful.

In 1982, as a result of the Frying Pan study, the State instigated its "Gold Medal Water" policy in which streams that would support a healthy wild fish population would no longer be stocked with catchable size trout, and special angling regulations would be in effect to maintain the fishing quality. Eight streams in the state as of 1986 are classified as "Gold Medal Water."

Currently the two miles of the Pan below Reudi Dam remain catch-and-release only, while the remainder of the river has a bag limit of one brown and one rainbow of any size. Except for children who may fish with bait, only artificial flies and lures may be used in the entire river.

Thanks to these special regulations, the fishing in the Frying Pan has improved considerably, and the river has become a prime example of the effectiveness of quality fishing regulations. Prior to the instigation of the special regulations, only 25 percent of the trout in the river were over twelve inches in length. However, after one year under the new regulations, more than 50 percent of the trout were over twelve inches long in the section of the river that was shocked.

The numbers and sizes of its fish are not the only things the Pan has going for it, though. The little river has an abundant insect population with hatches occurring in virtually every month of the year making it one of the few streams where an angler can combine dry fly fishing with a ski vacation.

During January and early February the air temperature may be below zero which, not too surprisingly, reduces the fishing pressure on the river considerably. However, the water being released from the dam maintains a fairly consistent temperature of forty-two to forty-three degrees Fahrenheit, and incredible midge hatches occur during this time. Hardy anglers willing to brave the cold will have lots of action on small (size 18-20), dark, quill bodied emergers fished right in the surface film with a 5-6X tippet. Pheasant Tail Nymphs in the film are also good, and Bill Fitzsimmons is particularly fond of a size 18 Adams tied with a rust colored tail which he believes may represent the nymphal shuck of the emerging adult.

The midge hatches continue until about April, and the best time to be on the river, according to Bill, is on the worst days — days that are fairly warm, but overcast and spitting snow. Under such conditions the water may be covered with hatching bugs, and fish will be rising everywhere. Bill suggests that if you're in the Aspen–Basalt area for skiing, ski on the bright days, but go fishing on the Pan on those days that really aren't the best for skiing anyway. When the light is flat and the weather nasty, the fish will be rising.

A few mayflies will start appearing in April — fairly dark *Baetis* — which can be matched with a size 18 Blue Winged Olive, Blue Dun, Quill Gordon or Blue Quill. Nymphs in the surface film or mahogany colored spinners will also be productive. During this time the fishing is best in the flatter sections of the river rather than in the pocket water.

The Blue Winged Olive is a standard pattern on the Pan, since the multi-brooded naturals are around most of the summer.

Depending upon the snow run off, a sulfur colored caddis comes off sometime around the end of May and into June. A size 14 to 16 down-wing pattern with a grey wing and orange–mustard colored body will fill the bill here.

Next, a size 14 to 16 Pale Morning Dun type of mayfly will appear and will hatch sparsely but steadily throughout the entire day — just the type of hatch that provides excellent fishing. During the remainder of the summer there is such an abundance of insect life on the river that almost any small dry fly will be effective.

The highlight of the summer, though, begins in August and lasts well into September, in a normal year, with the hatch of the Green Drakes. There is some disagreement over whether or not this is the *Drunell grandis* Green Drake that is typical in the West. Though the nymphs look similar to *D. grandis*, many of the adults do not, and there may even be two species masquerading as the Green Drake. Unfortunately, there has been little definitive entomological work done on the Pan.

Whatever the insect, a typical western Green Drake pattern in size 10 to 12 works very well for this important hatch. The insects will begin to come off the water about ten in the morning, and the big flies trickle off steadily all day. During the time of the Drakes, that is the only pattern needed to insure a great day of fishing.

In the fall, the water is low and clear, and the heaviest emergences of *Baetis* are seen. The big fish which were turned on to top water feeding by the Green Drakes remain active on the surface, and this is the best time to take really large fish on small flies. The fishing remains good right through the end of the year when it starts all over again!

Visiting anglers should be warned that, though there is plenty of public water, there is also quite a bit of private water on the Frying Pan. Be alert for posted sections of the river, and be sure to ask for permission to fish in these areas. A courteous request will often be rewarded.

The Frying Pan offers something for everyone. It is an excellent place for a beginning fly fisher because its size makes it very comfortable to fish and easy to read, and the abundance of twelve- to fourteen-inch trout insures success. The fish don't seem to be leader shy, and 3-4X tippets are adequate unless the small flies require going finer.

At the same time, the river provides a real challenge for those seeking the larger fish which are there — but are tougher to catch. And for the ultimate challenge, try ants and beetles fished near the banks in the Seven Castles stretch on a windy day. It's just like spring creek fishing to very difficult fish.

Incidentally, the Frying Pan isn't the only angling available in the area. Though the Roaring Fork is aptly named and is often out of shape during much of the year, it can also provide excellent fishing. Or, for a real change of pace, Bill Fitzsimmons' Taylor Creek Fly Shop in Basalt has arranged one-day and longer horse pack trips into the mountains for float tubing in the high lakes. Jeff and I spent a day on such a trip, and we had a great ride through some spectacular country, and very good float tube fishing in a pristine setting. It's a real Western adventure.

Accommodations are plentiful in the Aspen–Basalt area — more plentiful in Aspen, but less expensive in Basalt. The folks at the Aspenalt Motel (Best Western) in Basalt have given a 10 percent discount on rooms to TU members in the past. Aspen, of course, provides a wide range of activities for the entire family or can entertain the non-anglers while the others are out fishing.

A number of fly shops in Aspen and Glenwood Springs offer guide service on the Frying Pan, and in Basalt, the Pan flows right by the door of the Taylor Creek Fly Shop. Bill Fitzsimmons can provide guides, arrange horsepack trips, and provide up-to-the-minute information on the river [Taylor Creek Fly Shop, Basalt, Colorado 81621, Phone (303) 927-4374].

4.

Big Brookies of the Winisk

" . . . And the brook trout run to six or seven pounds," the voice on the other end of the telephone said casually. "Why don't you come up and join us?"

Now that got my full attention!

I don't know what it is about even the mere thought of big brook trout that stirs the imagination of anglers everywhere. Maybe it's their colorful beauty, or the remote regions to which one must travel to find them. Or it may be the fact that it's rare for most of us to ever catch a brookie that is more than twelve inches long. I suspect that it's probably the combination of all these things, but there is no doubt that the thought of brook trout measured in pounds rather than inches is exciting.

There was no need to waste time considering my decision, and I quickly accepted the invitation to join a small group of fishing writers for a fly-in trip to Ontario's Winisk River in search of big brook trout.

To most anglers, the life of a fishing writer is idyllic — it's a life of bright, sunny days, exotic places, leaping fish and screaming reels. Unfortunately, the reality is often quite different from the illusion.

I thought of that difference as I hunched cold and tired in the bow of the big canoe, and squinted into the driving, wind blown rain. While attempting to connect between two fishing trips, I had been stranded alone in a remote airport with nothing to read or eat for thirteen hours. I hadn't slept for thirty-six hours, and we still had several miles to go before we reached our first camp on the Winisk. If my readers could only see me now.

The rain turned to a light drizzle as we reached our camp, and by the time we'd finished eating dinner the evening sun was shining brightly. My thoughts were on a warm sleeping bag and a soft bed, but someone suggested, "Let's go fishing, it's a beautiful night!"

I had no choice but to join them.

My Ojibwa guide, Mathias Sugonaqueb, pushed our canoe into the water below Axe Handle Rapids. I opened my fly book and wondered what to try first. When I picked up a Black Marabou Leech, Mathias said, "Zusquajimae."

Not quite sure what I'd heard, I said, "What?"

"Zusquajimae," he replied. "That's 'black leech' in our language.

There's lots of them in here."

That settled that. I tied the weighted Black Leech onto a short leader ahead of a fast sinking 8-weight shooting head, and cast the fly into the dark, tea-colored water. Fatigue overrode my usual initial excitement when fishing new water, and I merely went through the motions of fishing.

I was half asleep when my fly abruptly stopped moving on its retrieve and I set the hook as pure reflex. Then I quickly woke up.

My fly rod took a deep bend, and a strong fish headed north for Hudson Bay.

The big fish ran, and dove and sulked, but finally was brought to Mathias' waiting net. Reaching into the net's large bag, I lifted out my first Winisk River brook trout. It weighed about four pounds, and was the largest brookie that I'd ever caught. My fatigue vanished. Maybe the perception of fishing writers was accurate after all.

The Winisk is a large, swift Ontario river that flows northward some two hundred miles from its origin into Hudson Bay. Wild and remote, the land along its entire length is designated a Provincial Wilderness Park. Near its headwaters, the Winisk flows past the small Ojibwa settlement of Webeque, a hundred miles from the nearest road, and the jump-off point for a guided trip down the magnificent river.

The natives of Webeque whose ancestors have hunted and fished in the region for many generations are the only licensed guides on the river. With the assistance of government development grants, and under the direction of Tom Shewaybick, the Band Chief, Peter Jacob, the Webeque Development Officer, and Mathias Sugonaqueb, the Band Administrator, their operation has become a model for other Canadian tribes.

Three permanent camps have been built along the river, each with a capacity of six guests plus guides. Each camp offers clean, well-screened plywood cabins, cooking facilities, and comfortable spring beds with foam mattresses. With the limited camp capacity, anglers are assured of virtually private fishing.

The Winisk is a series of long, flat pools interrupted by awesome, churning rapids. Traveling by twenty foot freight canoes powered by outboard motors, anglers and guides run down the quiet pools and either portage or line the boats down through the foaming rapids. Fishing is done below each set of rapids.

It was the size and speed of the water combined with my initial success with a fast sinking shooting head that led to my undoing during our first days on the Winisk. Everything in my experience told me that such conditions demand heavy, fast sinking tackle to get the fly down quickly to the depth of the fish. Thus, I resolutely stuck with my method even though the spin fishermen were taking considerably more fish than I. In fact, I had a frustrating dry spell of a day and a half while others were catching and releasing trout to six pounds.

When several of the others switched to fly tackle and continued to catch fish even though they only had sinking tip lines, I finally discovered what I should have learned long before—the fish weren't nearly as deep as I had expected. Though the spin fishermen were using heavy lures, the fast water was preventing them from getting very deep, and their fish had all been caught fairly close to the surface.

After I switched tackle and was into a good fish, Bob Rife yelled over to me above the roar of the rapids, "So, you finally got smart, huh?"

He was right. I had neglected my first rule of fishing. If you're not catching anything, experiment with different methods. The size of the water had so overwhelmed me that I failed to consider anything but what I "knew" was right, and it cost me some good fish.

In the days following my revelation, my luck improved considerably. Using an 8-weight sinking tip line and size 4 Muddler Minnows, Zonkers, leeches and stonefly nymphs I took fat brook trout up to about six pounds. Each fish was special, and I couldn't help but pause and admire its densely speckled back and rich pink and gold flanks before releasing it. Truly, the magnificence of the fish matched the country that was their home.

Though brook trout were our primary target, we also regularly caught walleye—pickerel, as the Canadians call them, and northern pike.

The stomach contents of the trout kept for the table indicated a rich food supply in the Winisk. Some trout were crammed full of small, dark nymphs, others were full of snails, while still others seemed to be feeding exclusively on small minnows and baitfish. Thus, the fly fisher can select from a wide range of suitable fly patterns. Muddler Minnows—originally developed in Ontario for big brookies, are probably the number one fly throughout the year, but other streamers and bucktails such as the Zonker, Black Nose Dace and Black Leech tied on size 4 hooks, are effective, too.

Nymph fishermen can do well with large, dark stoneflies, Wooly Buggers, and the Casual Dress.

Perhaps the key to success for fly fishermen on a large river such as the Winisk is to carry a selection of fly lines in a variety of sinking configurations. Weight forward floating, sinking tip, full sinking and shooting head lines allow the angler to meet any condition encountered. And take a tip from my sad experience, if one line doesn't produce, try something else.

The fish of the Winisk are not leader shy, and leaders do not need to be sophisticated. I prefer short leaders—say three feet or so, when I'm using a sinking line, to permit the fly to get down to the depth of the line. A nine foot leader works well when using a floating line with either dry or sunken flies. Tippets need be no finer than 2-3X.

During our trip in June we saw very little evidence of hatching insects, with the exception of a few caddis, and there was no significant surface feeding activity. However, according to Canadian writer Phil Kettle, who was with our group, and who has fished the Winisk later in the summer, excellent dry fly fishing is available during July and August. Phil, a past National President of Trout Unlimited, Canada, says that huge swarms of caddis often bring the big brookies to the surface, and a variety of Mayflies hatch during the late summer months. Big Humpies, Wulffs, and Irresistables, along with your favorite caddis dries, should produce well when the fish are on the surface.

The technique that produced the best for us was to cast well up into the fast water of the rapids and let the fly sweep down through the swift current. At the end of the drift, as it began to swing, the fly was retrieved with short, jerky strips. Strikes would often occur just at the end of the drift as the fly started its rise to the surface, or at any time during the retrieve.

The excellent fishing for large brook trout is what brings anglers to the Winisk, but it is the people of Webeque who make it all happen. Without exception, the friendly townspeople and guides went out of their way to help us in any way possible. The guides exhibited a sense of humor often lacking in such situations, and they were extremely competent on the river.

An example of the attitude of the townspeople to visiting anglers is seen in an experience that happened while we were waiting for the plane that was to take us home at the end of our trip. Our group trooped up to the small craftshop and store to buy souvenirs — handmade leather gloves, purses and moccasins made by the Ojibwa. I spotted a painting done in the stylized manner of the tribe on the wall of the coffee shop, and asked Andrew, the proprietor, if there was anyone in town who sold paintings.

"Yes," he replied, I think so," and he disappeared into the kitchen.

Nothing more was said, and I was wondering what had happened, when Andrew appeared and told us to go over to the tribal office building where someone would have a painting. Unbeknownst to us, he had put out a call over the small local radio station, and when we arrived at the office building many craftsman had gathered with their work.

There was a mad scramble as we all began to make our choices and bargain in sign language with those who spoke no English. I spotted an old woman holding a paper bag and standing back from the crowd. When I motioned to her, she smiled a toothless grin and reached into the bag to remove the only painting anyone had brought — a colorful brook trout against the traditional Ojibwa symbol for the sun. The painting now hangs in my fly tying room as a constant reminder of the big trout of the Winisk and the friendly Ojibwa of Webeque.

Big brook trout are, indeed, rare and exciting and found only in exotic places. But the fish and the place are within reach of anyone who has ever dreamed of them on Ontario's beautiful Winisk River.

How To Book

The fishing season in the Winisk Wilderness Camps runs from June 1st to September 15, with the best fishing likely to be found after mid-July.

Booking information can be obtained by writing to: Winisk Wilderness Camps, P.O. Box 1230, Waterdown, Ontario, Canada L0R 2H0. Telephone: (416) 689-7925.

The usual departure points for Webeque are either Thunder Bay or Geraldton, Ontario, where air service is provided by Austin Airways. Flight arrangements can be made with Winisk Wilderness Camps when the trip is booked.

Two meal plans are available at the Winisk Camps—the housekeeping plan in which anglers provide their own food and do their own cooking, and the American plan in which these services are provided by the guides. If you plan to supply your own food, it is best to purchase it in Webeque, since you are limited to 44 pounds of baggage for your flight. The food bought in Webeque will prove more economical than the high cost of excess baggage for hauling it in from the outside.

Summer weather in northern Canada can vary from hot to cool, and wool shirts or sweaters and rain gear are in order. Anglers are expected to provide their own sleeping bags and towels. Since there is no electricity in the camps, bring along a flashlight and lantern, if desired. Blackflies can be heavy in July and early August, so take plenty of bug dope, mosquito coils, and possibly a headnet. A limited amount of spinning tackle, lures and line can be purchased in Webeque, but no fly fishing tackle is available.

5.

Alberta's Beautiful Bow

To me, almost any fishing trip is special. But a trip with one of my sons to a magnificent river in Canada in early September, when the cottonwoods are turning to gold, thousands of geese are migrating across clear blue skies, and three to four pound trout come readily to the fly, is very, very special.

My oldest son, Eric, and I took just such a trip some years ago, and it was special, indeed.

Due to college and his summer jobs, Eric and I had had few opportunities to fish together for some time, and invariably at some point during our long distance phone conversations, he would say, "I sure wish we could go fishing!" I felt the same way, and I was determined to put together an adventure that neither of us would ever forget. When the opportunity to travel to Alberta's Bow River arose, I knew that I had found the trip that I was waiting for.

I had heard rumblings about the Bow for several years. Nothing too specific was ever said, and I'm not certain that I had ever talked with anyone who had actually fished the river. But the rumors always sounded interesting. In fact, they sounded almost too good to be true.

The rainbow and brown trout were supposed to be very large, they were supposed to take the fly eagerly, and the river was supposed to be very much under-fished. It sounded like an angler's pipe dream; a fly fisher's Shangrila.

Now, in retrospect, I know that the rumors were probably not strong enough in their praise of the river, for the Bow proved to be the best single trout stream that it has ever been my pleasure to fish.

The Bow arises from Bow Lake in Canada's Banff National Park high in the rugged Rockies. As it flows down out of the mountains it is a typical high country freestone stream populated by whitefish, a limited number of insects, and a few brown trout. When it reaches the prairie below, it changes little until it reaches the city of Calgary some fifty miles to the southeast.

At Calgary, an incredible change occurs in the river, and for the next forty miles the Bow becomes nothing less than a fly fisher's paradise.

Ironically, this change is due to the city itself. A city of 600,000 people, Calgary dumps much of its waste into the Bow. To be sure, the waste has received primary and secondary treatment, and the river is in no way an open sewer, but sufficient nutrients remain to tremendously enrich the water. Aquatic insects and flora flourish, and trout grow very large.

There are those who object to the "sewage" in the Bow. The thought of it is not very appealing. But the river is not polluted, and the angler is not aware of the source of its richness. It looks like nothing but the beautiful trout stream that it is. And without Calgary, the Bow would be just another river.

It is possible to begin fishing the Bow right in the heart of downtown Calgary, for the river is flanked on either side by Fish Creek Park, the largest urban park in Canada. Drifting anglers can take husky trout practically within shouting distance of the busy city — and they won't even be aware that it's there.

For our first day's float, though, we launched our Jon boat at the southern city limit, on what could only be described as an ideal fall day. The air was crisp, the sky a deep blue, and the first tinges of gold were beginning to color the big cottonwoods that lined the river. As Rick Harding, our guide, suggested, we rigged two outfits each. One, a light 5-6 weight rod with a floating line, a ten foot leader tapered to 4X, and fitted with a size 16 or 18 Adams dry fly. The second rod was a little heavier — a 7-8 weight, also fitted with a floating line, but with a size 4 white marabou streamer attached to the 2X tippet.

The plan — typical for the Bow — was to drift and cast the streamers close to the edges of the weed beds that line the river at this time of year. Then, when we spotted surface activity, we would beach the boat, switch rods, and fish dry.

As usual when starting to fish a new river, we were excited as we began to drift with the smooth, steady current. The clean, clear water looked very fishy. As instructed, we cast our streamers toward the weeds, and stripped them back in short rapid twitches. So often, though, the initial excitement of a new river is short-lived when the fish fail to cooperate. But not this time. Before we had drifted a hundred yards, a large boil engulfed my darting fly, the rod tip jerked downward, and I felt the solid take of a large fish. Surprised by the sudden action, I missed it.

That fish was all that was needed to put me into the proper frame of mind, though, and when the next one hit a few yards farther downstream, I was ready. When finally boated, the chunky rainbow weighed about two and a half pounds. It was deep bodied, and very strong. Then it was Eric's turn, and after a lengthy battle punctuated by his shouts and the fish's twisting leaps, he boated the twin to my fish.

The action slowed a little after the initial flurry, and we drifted lazily downstream enjoying the day, the passing scenery and an occasional fish. Rick lamented the fact that the fishing was really fairly slow compared to what one would normally expect during the second week in September, but we found it difficult to consider it such.

Both browns and rainbows had come to our flies. We caught nothing under about a pound and a half, and took a number of fish of between three and four pounds. In every case, the fish were very deep bodied and were the hardest fighting trout that I had ever caught. One rainbow was especially so. At eighteen inches in length, the chubby fish weighed about three and a half pounds, and, according to the guides, was the heaviest fish of its length they had ever seen in the Bow. By any standard, we had had a very good day of fishing — and we had seen no other anglers.

As mentioned earlier, the Bow is an incredibly rich stream. A study conducted in 1978 estimated that the weed growth exceeded 70 tons per mile of river bottom, and as might be expected, such lush vegetation produces an abundant supply of insect life as food for the fish. Thus, it is not surprising that the trout grow fat, strong, and scrappy in the Bow.

The native fish in the Bow were cutthroat, and apparently brown trout were introduced to the system by accident around 1925. Between 1929 and 1938 cutthroat were stocked in the river, and in 1939 rainbows were introduced. Gradually, however, the cutts were replaced by the non-native species, and now the river below Calgary yields roughly 75 percent rainbows and 25 percent browns. For many years, it has been Alberta's policy not to stock fish in waters capable of sustaining natural reproduction, and today the trout in the Bow are wild fish.

A study conducted in 1981 on the 9.5 mile stretch of river immediately below Calgary found a population of 1,296 rainbows and 465 brown trout per mile, and the investigator indicated that these figures might be low as representing the populations of the entire forty miles of prime trout water. And, in addition to the numbers of fish, current figures indicate that their growth rate is better than that of Montana's Madison River, and is on a par with the Big Horn — a fact that is especially remarkable since the Big Horn was closed to all fishing for five years prior to the 1981 study.

Statistics on the fish caught in the Bow are equally impressive. Figures compiled from the 1980 guiding records of Jim McLennan of the Country Pleasures Orvis shop in Calgary indicate that 58 percent of the fish caught by clients were over fifteen inches in length, and 23 percent were over eighteen inches long. In contrast, only 12 percent were less than twelve inches in length. According to Jim, these figures are still probably quite representative, or if anything, a little low.

In addition to the richness of the river and the numbers and sizes of the fish, the Bow is unusual in another way. It is, in effect, two rivers in one. The first river is the Bow of the early season — a typical freestone stream that is high, off color and with little weed growth. During the month of June the river is best fished with heavy tackle — an 8-9 weight rod with sinking lines and heavily weighted leeches and streamers. Though the conditions are not ideal, the angler who fishes deep and slowly will be rewarded with some large trout.

By July, the water clears and drops, and the second Bow appears with the characteristics of a huge spring creek. Then the first surface activity begins, streamers are still effective, and the fishing is more varied. By mid-July, the Pale Morning Duns (size 16) which began hatching sporadically in late June have started to emerge in tremendous numbers, and the fish's interest is drawn to the surface.

At this time anglers have, perhaps, their best opportunities to take trout of over twenty inches on dry flies. Fish of twenty-three inches are fairly common, and twenty-four inchers are not unusual. Anything larger than that is pretty special. Bow River trout of twenty-one inches can be expected to weigh in at about four pounds.

In early August the *Tricorythodes* start to emerge, as does the little Blue Winged Olive. The Tricos can be matched by any of the standard size 20-22 Black and White Spinner patterns, while a size 18 Adams will usually suffice for the Blue Winged Olives. In addition to these insects of major importance, heavy hatches of a variety of caddis will be on the water from late June to mid-August, and 'hoppers will be abundant from mid-August through the fall. The Blue Winged Olives often continue to hatch right through until the end of the season in October. Late season anglers also will find large attractor patterns, such as size 8-10 Royal Wulffs, effective.

Even during the peak of the dry fly season, the knowledgeable Bow River angler will generally rig both a dry and a streamer outfit, and will fish below the surface until rising fish are located. But, as Jim McLennan says, "Sometimes the dry flies are so hot that we don't even bother to set up a streamer rod."

When asked to name the prime time to be on the Bow, Rick replied, "Well, I guess that would have to be either the second week of July or the second week of September." Jim agreed, and Eric and I just laughed — the date was September 9th, and we had an entire week ahead of us!

Each day Rick or Jim would pick us up at our hotel in Calgary, and we'd drive out across the flat Alberta wheat country to a new section of the river. It didn't look like trout country, and there was no indication that there was a trout stream within a hundred miles — just wheat fields and cattle.

We'd turn off the highway, drive a while on a back road, and suddenly the road would drop into an unseen canyon. There, spread out before us, would be the Bow and a whole different world. Stands of tall cottonwood trees and rocky cliffs lined the river, broken here and there by lush meadows, and wildlife was everywhere.

The cackle of geese would fill the air as long skeins of the big Honkers made their way South. Ducks and shore birds cruised the shallows and strutted on the sandy beach, and mink would scamper for cover at our approach. As our Jon boat drifted down the river, muskrats and beaver would slip silently into the water, and whitetail

On the Bow River.

or mule deer would stand in the shadows and watch us glide by. Once, a huge bald eagle erased all thoughts of fishing from our minds as we watched it soar high overhead. Yes, the Bow may well have been Shangrila during the second week of September.

So we'd drift down the river casting our streamers toward the weeds, enjoying the scenery and wildlife, and giving whoops of pure joy when an outsized brown or rainbow would attack our offerings. Occasionally we'd pull the boat onto a beach and stalk up a narrow side channel or along one of the guide's favorite riffles scanning the water for the sipping rises of feeding trout.

It was on such a stop that Jim and Eric spotted the dimples made by a string of four rainbows actively feeding about six inches off the grassy bank of a narrow channel beside a long island. It was Eric's first attempt at such demanding angling, and he waded carefully into the water below the busy trout. Again and again he gently dropped his little Adams above the lower fish until finally a small ring encircled the fly and the fish sucked it in.

Fifteen minutes later the second 'bow accepted his offering.

Anxious to get in on the action, I moved on up the channel and spotted a rise of my own to work, but before I took the fish Eric had his third. His three rainbows weighed two to three pounds each, and when I finally took mine it was about two and a half pounds.

Eric continued to work the last of the fish he had found, while I fished on up to the end of the channel and then walked back to the boat. Evening was approaching, and at last I called to Eric, "We'd better get going, it's getting late."

"O.K., I'll be right there."

Ten minutes passed, and still I could see Eric's rod waving back and forth on the other side of the island's tall grass.

"Eric, let's go!"

"In a minute."

"Eric!"

Silence.

"Eric!!"

More silence.

Then, *Splash*! "I got him, Dad! *Wow*!"

And the sound of a singing reel filled the air.

His patience had paid off. The fish was the largest of the four.

A new spring creek fisherman had been born. And it was a happy kid and a mighty proud father who finally climbed back into the boat.

Except for occasional wind, the weather during our stay on the Bow was ideal. While the evening might see frost, daytime temperatures in September can be expected to be between sixty-five and seventy degrees Fahrenheit. During July and August the daytime average will be between seventy-five and eighty-five degrees with highs of ninety degrees possible. The evenings may drop into the fifties.

In an attempt to maintain the quality of the fishery, more stringent regulations became effective in 1983. In the forty miles of water below Calgary, all fish over 40 centimeters (15¾ inches) must be released. The creel limit is two trout, and no bait of any kind may be used.

Almost as noticeable as the abundant wildlife along the river was the complete lack of other anglers. Although this was reputed to be one of the two best times to fish the Bow, we saw only one other boat during our week of floating. I suppose that for most fly fishers the summer holidays were over, the kids were back in school, and thoughts were turning to other matters, but it was hard to imagine why such a magnificent river that is so close to over a half a million people would be so empty of anglers. I understand that July and August are a little more crowded, though, as the river is popular with local canoeists, particularly on weekends.

The foregoing is the good news about the Bow. The bad news is that public access and boat launching sites are quite limited on the river. The Provincial government is attempting to improve the river's accessibility, but as of 1986, boats can enter and leave the water at only a few locations. Unfortunately, the problem is further complicated by the lack of maps indicating where launching is possible.

Floating with a guide, of course, solves the access problem, and is probably the best way to learn the river. Anglers who plan to float on their own, would do well to check with Jim McLennan and the boys at Country Pleasures, the Orvis shop in Calgary. They'll draw you maps, and give you up-to-date information on the river. Those looking for guide service should make reservations in advance, since there are only a limited number of guides working in the river.

Obviously, the Bow River holds many attractions for anglers, but those whose families also have some non-fishing members should consider the Calgary area as the spot for a great family vacation, too. The activities of the city will entertain the non-anglers while the others are plying the Bow for a few days, and when the fishing is finished, a great side trip awaits the entire family.

Just an hour or so to the west of Calgary, the awesome Canadian Rockies, and the Banff and Jasper National Parks offer scenery and excitement for everyone. After leaving the Bow, Eric and I drove to Banff and on up to Lake Louise where we lunched in the stately Lake Louise Chateau overlooking the lake and its picturesque glacier.

We then drove up the Trans-Canada Highway 93 to spend the night in Jasper. Along the way we hiked up the Athabasca Glacier, counted elk and deer, and came to understand why the road has the reputation of being one of the most magnificent drives in the world. Every bend of the highway provided a new vista of jagged peaks and icy glaciers, and the farther north we drove, the more beautiful the fall colors became.

It was a fitting end to our adventure.

For further information contact Country Pleasures #570 Willow Park Village, 10816 Macloud Trail, Calgary, Alberta T2J 5N8. [Phone: (403) 271-1023].

6.

Alaska:
A Fly Fisher's Paradise

S uppose for a moment that, like a modern day Moses, you were called to a high mountain top, and a thunderous voice from the clouds commanded you to design a remote corner of the world especially for fly fishermen. There would be no restrictions, and your imagination could run wild. The only requirement would be that the result of your efforts had to provide the world's best fly fishing.

How would you begin?

Being serious about your sport and knowing how popular fly fishing is becoming, you'd probably want a rather large area — let's make it twice as big as the state of Texas or about one-fifth the total area of the continental United States. Of course, there would have to be plenty of water, a dozen major river drainages is a nice round number, and would provide many thousands of miles of clear streams. Then, for good measure, you could toss in at least seven million acres of lakes.

There would have to be a wide variety of fish to satisfy every taste — you could start with five different kinds of salmon and add some Arctic grayling, Arctic charr, Dolly Varden trout, rainbow trout, and lake trout, and polish off the assortment with northern pike, whitefish, and inconnu. That should provide plenty of interest for everyone.

There would have to be a wide range of scenery, too, so you'd probably want to include magnificent snow capped peaks in ranges, icy glaciers, mile after mile of thick forests, and for variety, an abundance of lush tundra. And a land such as this should be filled with wildlife, so you'd want to add black, brown, and grizzly bear, moose, wolves, deer, caribou, and a myriad of small animals. The clear blue sky should be filled with birds — you could start with regal bald eagles and elegant swans, and fill the rest of the spaces with almost every feathered creature you could name. And, for spice, let's cover the ground with a complete rainbow of wild flowers.

Finally, so paradise shouldn't be too crowded, let's only give it about 400,000 people. That would work out to something like two thirds of a person per square mile, but we can put half of those into one large city to give the rest of us even more room in which to play.

That should about do it. Kind of a nice daydream, wasn't it?

Did I say a daydream? Well, it may have been for us, but someone must have gone through exactly that process at sometime, because such a place really does exist. It's called Alaska, and it's a fly fisher's paradise.

For those who haven't been there, it's difficult to imagine the fantastic quantity and quality of fly fishing that is available in our forty-ninth state. Other places may provide the opportunity to catch very large fish of one or two species, but I know of nowhere else that provides the broad scope of fresh water fishing that is found in Alaska.

Visiting anglers have essentially three options when planning an Alaska fly fishing adventure. They can drive from a number of cities and camp beside a stream or lake. They can charter a float plane to drop them into a lake or stream in the wilderness, where they can camp as long as they wish and then be picked up at a pre-determined time. Or, they can make reservations at a commercial lodge in the area they wish to fish. Each option has its own advantages and disadvantages.

Of the three choices, the first is perhaps the most economical, and with careful planning, can prove an exciting trip. Unfortunately, this is not the way to find the best fishing. Since most of Alaska is remote wilderness, there are relatively few roads outside of the "urban" areas, and the waters that are available by highway receive a considerable amount of fishing pressure. Even in Alaska the waters close to town will be crowded.

On the other hand, if you should want to combine fishing with sight-seeing and you have time, you can plan to ride an Alaska ferry boat up the inland waterway from Seattle and maybe even drive the Alcan Highway back home. Such a trip would provide excellent scenery, a real sense of adventure, and a goodly number of fishing opportunities. The trip should be thoroughly planned well in advance, though, as reservations are required for the ferry, and your car should be well prepared for the rigors of the Alcan Highway. In fact, it would probably be best to drive to Alaska and relax after your trip with the ferry boat ride back home. Of course, anglers who wish to drive to their fishing can also fly to one of Alaska's cities and rent a car for the duration of their stay.

The second option, chartering a float plane to drop you at a remote campsite for a designated length of time, may provide better fishing, since you can get well into the backcountry and away from the crowds. Many charter flying services are available in almost every Alaskan community, and most of them will offer suggestions on where to find good fishing.

This method, too, is not without its drawbacks, however. You may well find excellent fishing, but since you will be pretty well locked into one particular location, you could be stuck on an unproductive piece of water for your entire trip. And if the weather should be bad, the plane is unable to land to pick you up on time, or a bear destroys your camp, the stay could be miserable, indeed.

This leaves the third, and probably the best, option, the commercial lodge. While this represents the most expensive of the three alternatives, it is also one of the safest to insure good fishing. Such lodges will be one of two types. The first will be located on good fishing water, and most fishing will be by boat on day trips from the lodge. The second type may or may not be on good fishing water, but will feature daily fly-out trips in float equipped planes.

Because of the great range of the float planes, and their ability to go where the fish are, the fly-out lodge will often provide the best and most flexible fishing opportunities. It will also be the most expensive, and there is always the possibility that poor weather will ground the planes. In such cases, many fly-out lodges can provide fishing by boat close to home.

Due to the high cost of keeping a fleet of float planes in the air, an angler visiting a fly-out lodge can expect to pay from two to three thousand dollars per week, not including transportation to the lodge's pick-up point. There is simply no way to take such a trip inexpensively. However, when considering the cost of even the least expensive Alaskan trip, the extra charge for a fly-out lodge may well be worth every penny, considering the increased odds of finding outstanding fishing.

Typical of the fly-out lodges is the Bristol Bay Lodge. Located on Lake Aleknagik about three hundred air miles southwest of Anchorage in the heart of the famed Wood River–TikChik Lakes area, Bristol Bay Lodge offers first class accommodations and outstanding fly fishing. At a lodge of this type, anglers can expect fine meals, knowledgeable guides, and a pleasant, relaxed atmosphere.

At Bristol Bay and most other fly-out lodges, the usual procedure is to decide each evening what species you want to fish for the next day, where you will go, and who will be in your party. Following a hearty breakfast the next morning, the groups disperse to their selected sites, fish all day with time out for a shore lunch, and fly back to the lodge in the late afternoon. In the rare event that the fishing is off that day at your first location, it is a simple matter to fly somewhere else in search of more productive water. Thus, the fly-out angler considerably increases the odds of finding superb fishing.

While there is usually excellent fishing all season, the species you will be after depends, in part, upon when you are there. The exact dates will vary depending upon your location in Alaska, but typically king salmon (chinook) will be in the rivers from mid-June through July. These powerful fish can reach fifty pounds and are a real challenge on fly fishing tackle. From late June through August, the sockeye (red) salmon move into the fresh water. Running to as much as fifteen pounds, the reds are extremely active when "fresh" and may well be the best of all the salmon on the table.

The chum (dog) and pink (humpy) salmon will be found in the rivers from mid-July through mid-August, and while these two species don't enjoy the reputation of the other salmon, they can be excellent sport on flies.

Finally, the silver salmon (coho) start moving in mid-August and continue well into September. The silvers will run to fifteen pounds and average a little better than ten pounds, and they take a fly readily. Many anglers consider them to be *the* salmon for the fly fisherman in Alaska.

Along with the salmon, grayling, Arctic charr, Dolly Varden, rainbow trout and northern pike will be available all season. The prime times for big rainbow in the ten pound plus class are June and September.

Since the fish, flies, and many of the waters will be large, fairly heavy tackle is in order. The best all-around rod for Alaskan fishing is probably one of eight to nine feet in length which balances with a number eight line. Such a rod will handle most fish under most of the conditions you will face. If you plan to fish king salmon, you might also want to take a ten weight outfit, and if you're after grayling, a five or six weight outfit will provide more sport. Reels should carry *at least* one hundred yards of 18-25 pound test dacron backing.

One of the keys to successful fly fishing in Alaska is to carry a good selection of lines. Effective fishing depends upon getting the fly in front of the fish under a wide range of water depths and current speeds. Sinking tip, sinking head, and sinking belly lines in both fast and extra fast sink rates can be very helpful, and for convenience, many anglers use a variety of shooting heads in front of .029 inch level floating running line. Floating lines will also be needed for greyling, northern pike, and much of the rainbow trout fishing. In all cases, a weight forward taper will assist with long casts under windy conditions.

Except for grayling where lighter tippets are called for, leaders should tip out at 8-15 pounds depending upon the size of the fish and the flies. When fishing sinking lines, leaders can be simple affairs consisting of only a butt section and a tippet, and they should be kept very short. I have found it convenient to permanently attach a 10-inch piece of .021-inch monofilament to the tip of the fly line, tie a loop into this leader butt, and then attach the required tippet to the loop. A short leader of this type will allow the fly to get deep quickly, and it will ride at the depth of the line rather than considerably higher as with a long leader.

Since Alaskan fish are not generally selective feeders, fly patterns can be rather simple, also. For all species of salmon, bucktail patterns, which represent small baitfish, are particularly effective. I like to tie mine on stainless steel saltwater hooks with a braided mylar piping body and a wing of green or blue bucktail or FisHair over white. Yellow and red also make good color combinations. They can range from two to four inches in length. Various "egg" type patterns, such as the Tulley Polar Shrimp, Babine Special, Two Egg Sperm and the Egg and I, are effective for the charr and the Dolly Varden, which feed on the salmon spawn, and they will take salmon as well.

The bucktails will also be effective for rainbows, and in shallow water streams it's hard to beat a greased Muddler Minnow (size 4-8) on a floating line. Grayling can be taken on typical trout type dry flies in sizes 12 to 18, as well as nymphs. An assortment of black, brown, and grey flies should do the trick. Big bucktails are also good for northern pike, but for real sport, try big bass bugs on a floating line. My favorite is a deer hair mouse which will bring savage strikes when swum through pike water. In addition to the above, most lodges will have favorite local patterns, and they will usually be happy to supply you with a fly list before your trip or the flies themselves when you get there.

Alaskan weather can be delightfully warm in the summertime with temperatures sometimes reaching the mid-eighties. However, that far north, it can also be very cool, especially early and late in the season. Therefore, it is well to be prepared with clothing that will keep you comfortable at either extreme. Rain is a distinct possibility at any time, and good rain gear is a must. Since many of the river bottoms can be slippery, some type of wading sandals featuring cleats or spikes can provide much needed extra traction and save a spill in heavy, cold water.

Most fishing camps in Alaska are very remote, therefore, extra fishing tackle will often be difficult to come by, and when it is available it will be expensive. Thus, the wise angler will bring an extra rod or two, spare lines, leader material, flies, wader repair kit, and anything else that may be lost or broken. It would be a good idea to check ahead of time as to just what items may be available at the lodge.

While most Alaskan lodges cater to fly fishermen, not all do, and some have relatively little experience guiding fly fishermen. When selecting a lodge, it is a good idea to ask some pertinent questions in this respect to be assured of a good experience when you arrive. If you can't find a friend who has visited a lodge you are considering, most reputable camps will provide a list of references, and it would be an excellent idea to contact someone who has fished there. A little preliminary investigation can head off potential problems.

Anglers considering a trip to Alaska would also do well to purchase the book *How to Catch Alaska's Trophy Sportfish* by Chris Batin. (Alaska Angler Publications, P.O. Box 8-3550, Fairbanks, AK 99708. $19.95). This book, while not aimed specifically at the fly fisherman, contains a wealth of information on all aspects of fishing and travel in Alaska. It's well worth reading and having as a reference.

As this is being written, I can look up at the bookcase above my desk and see a bumper sticker that says, "I'd Rather Be Fishing Alaska." And I guess that would be true regardless of what I was doing. Our forty-ninth state is a place of magnificent beauty, friendly people, and outstanding fly fishing. It is truly a fly fisherman's paradise.

7.

Oregon's Williamson River

The conversation had begun to lag at our table of tired fishermen, and the waitress was refilling my coffee cup for the third time when Richard Henry inquired innocently, "Dave, you've fished many famous rivers around the world. Have you ever seen anything like the Williamson?"

I didn't answer right away, but sipped at the steaming cup of coffee and recalled the many places I'd been privileged to fish. I considered the big rivers and the small streams I'd seen, the fish, the hatches, and the subtle character of the waters. Finally I took one more swallow of coffee and answered, "No, I don't think I've ever seen another river quite like the Williamson."

I had heard rumors of Oregon's Williamson River long before I fished it. For several years its name had cropped up occasionally when friends and I were sitting on the banks of some remote stream or around a campfire chatting about the things fly fisherman chat about. But, usually, not much was said. Most often, mention of the Williamson would bring knowing smiles from those who had fished it, while the rest of us would sit with the blank looks that bespeak ignorance. Mention of the river was made often enough to begin to make me very curious.

Ultimately it happened — the last straw. I was wandering around a sportsman's show, halfheartedly glancing at the myriad of booths one last time when I picked up the tag end of someone's conversation. All I heard was the word "Williamson," but it was enough to jerk me back to life and make me look around to see where the word had come from.

It didn't take long to work my way into the conversation or to meet the speaker, Chad Carroll. A big, friendly bear of a man, Chad thrust out a huge paw to shake my hand and exclaimed, "You've never fished the Williamson? Man, you don't know what you're missing!"

Carroll went on to describe the river passionately and I took it all in — but with a grain of salt, for I'd heard such descriptions before. As he told me about his guide service on the Williamson, Chad shoved his business card toward me. It was Day-Glo orange, which somehow seemed appropriate. But my mind was made up — I would pay Chad Carroll and the Williamson River a visit.

And so it was that I found myself late one July night drinking coffee with Chad, Randy Sparacino and Richard Henry at a truck stop just outside of Chiloquin, Oregon. We had spent several evenings on the Williamson, and I had indeed never seen anything quite like it.

The Williamson begins as a clear, cold spring creek on the Yamsay Ranch about thirty river miles north of Chiloquin. After flowing through the Klamath Marsh and gaining volume from numerous other springs, the river bends south toward Chiloquin and Klamath Lake. Six or seven miles above Chiloquin, the Williamson is joined by Spring Creek which further increases its volume, and finally, just below the Chiloquin Bridge, it merges with the Sprague River and achieves its full size.

At their confluence, the Williamson and the Sprague form a huge mixing bowl of a pool called the Blue Hole. Access is limited to the Williamson, and the public launch site at Blue Hole is the usual take-off point for a float of the section below Chiloquin.

For my first look at the river, Chad, Randy, Rich and I prepared to launch two drift boats at the Blue Hole late one afternoon, and it quickly became clear that this was not a typical Western river. The Blue Hole plunged to an unseen depth that I could only guess at. Huge boulders and submerged rock shelves projected from the shadows and my pulse quickened as I considered the size fish such water could hold.

We were rigging our tackle before boarding the boats and I had just fitted a spool of fast-sinking line into my reel when Rich casually suggested that I might want to replace my leader with a longer one. He suggested twelve feet tapered to 4X. In recent years I've usually found myself tying on three-foot long leaders when using sinking lines, as this seems to help keep the fly near the bottom where I want it. I protested mildly, but did as I was told. I long ago discovered the wisdom of taking a guide's advice when fishing unfamiliar water.

Chad handed me a supply of long, slinky olive and black marabou leeches like the ones the others had already secured to their tippets. The flies were a good three or four inches long, lightly weighted, and tied on turned-up eye, low-water style, size 4 to 6 Partridge salmon fly hooks. These hooks, Chad explained, are very sharp, have a short front point and a wide gap, all of which improves their hooking ability. The flies were considerably different from my heavily weighted leeches, which were tied on standard hooks, and I took the proffered samples gratefully. A guide's advice should not be ignored.

I had listened all afternoon to my three guides swapping tales of the river and its fish. Colorful names for their favorite pools had sprinkled the conversation—Jailhouse Pool, Bathtub Hole, Stinking Horse Hole, the Log Hole and the Slaughter House. Rich's eyes nearly glazed over when he told of his favorite adversaries—Big Mamoo and Freight Train—outsized rainbow trout that he had hooked on numerous occasions. I was ready to fish when we finally pushed out onto the river.

A few quick casts into the Blue Hole brought no results, and we let the boats drift downstream in the steady current. Brush and rock outcrops lined both banks of the broad river, and an occasional riffle contributed to its character. Here and there I could see the huge slabs of submerged rock ledges beneath the surface. Or I'd notice a slot of fast water swirling into a still, deep pool. This was big fish water.

At last we let the boats slide in close to a brushy bank and dropped the anchors to position the boats a few feet off the willows. We had reached a special pool that the guides had been waiting for and suddenly the fishing became very serious.

Fortunately Randy had warned me about Rich's skill and had suggested that I pay close attention to his technique. I did as I was told and received a lesson I won't soon forget. First I noticed that Rich's casts were not random. Quartering downstream, his leech seemed to drop consistently at the exact spot he wanted beside a particular limb on the bank. Then he would sit quietly and enjoy the sights of the river before starting his retrieve. Or so it appeared. It didn't take long to realize that his seeming nonchalance was anything but — he was counting as the fly sank to precisely the depth he wanted. Only then did he begin his retrieve.

Standing in the boat, Rich would place the tip of his rod right down on the water's surface, and with an almost palsied twitch of his wrist would produce a very short, quick stripping retrieve. It was a technique he had developed during many hours on the river and I was fascinated to watch the beauty and efficiency of it.

I was spellbound, but the spell was broken when Rich gave a loud laugh and vigorously lifted his rod to set the hook. And I doubt that I have ever seen anyone enjoy playing a fish as much. Rich's laugh continued to punctuate a running conversation with the powerful fish. When the fish sulked Rich tried to cajole it back into action, and when the reel sang he would match it note for note. When brought to net, the broad bright rainbow weighed in at something over four pounds.

That fish set the tone of the trip: the scene was repeated numerous times that night and the next. We would find *exactly* the right spot to place the anchor, let out precisely the correct amount of anchor line, make very accurate casts, and let the fly sink to the appropriate depth for that specific pool. Very little was left to chance.

By the end of the first night of fishing, Rich had landed six rainbows from four to seven pounds each. Randy had taken a couple in the same range, and I had come away with nothing but several savage hits that I missed completely.

The second evening was a carbon copy of the first — except that Rich's fish got bigger. (His largest was 9½ pounds.) Randy's fish were about the same size as the previous night, and mine were, again, missed strikes.

During these two evenings, we had seen only one or two local anglers fishing from the river banks; there had been no boats. For a river of its size and with its potential for such large trout, the Williamson has been greatly under-fished.

Richard Henry is a legend on the Williamson, and after watching him, it's easy to see why. A native Klamath Indian, Rich grew up on the Williamson and has probably spent more time fly-fishing it than any other man alive. Hours spent underwater with scuba gear have taught him the river bottom in intimate detail. He knows where the fish lie, where they move, and what they feed on. He has honed his angling skills to perfection in pursuit of the big Williamson browns and rainbow. According to Randy, Rich spends 361 days a year fishing and the other four days traveling. It shows in his results.

I learned a great deal from fishing with Richard Henry, not the least of which was the necessity of having a guide when fishing the Williamson. Without one, it would be difficult either to locate the fish or to adapt your technique to the special requirements of the river. In addition, the Williamson has only limited public access, and floating is the only reasonable way to adequately cover the water. A guide solves both problems.

As we fished the Williamson, I learned why my guides had suggested a modification of both my leader and my leech pattern. Much of the time we were fishing over a bottom covered with a lush growth of weeds. Had I used my short nymph leader and a heavily-weighted pattern, my fly would have sunk into the weeds and gotten hung up. By lengthening the leader and using a lightly weighted pattern, I could keep the fly riding just above the submerged weeds even though the fast-sinking line itself was down among them. Rich also believes that the longer leader lets the fly drift more naturally in the subtle currents near the river bottom. This terminal gear, combined with an accurate "count-down" tailored to each pool and the correct short strip retrieve of the fly, considerably increases an angler's chances of taking big fish.

No...I didn't land a single fish, but I learned from a master and was rewarded with a number of lost fish. I made progress.

According to my guides, the unusual water conditions of that season produced particularly difficult late-July fishing. The short-nosed suckers had spawned later than usual, and the big fish that normally move up from Klamath Lake were holding lower in the river to feed on sucker eggs. Also, the Williamson's normally cold spring-fed water depends on warmer water entering from the Sprague River to bring it into the ideal trout temperature range. That year low water in the Sprague delayed this warming effect. In a typical year, the fishing should be considered better and easier.

During early season (June) the best fishing is found upstream where Spring Creek enters the Williamson. The Log Hole, Bathtub, Slaughter House and Old Corral Pools are favorite spots, as is the long stretch of beautiful dry-fly water below Collier Park. Collier Park provides a public launch site for a float of this portion of the river. When the water is dark and coffee-colored, the confluence of Spring Creek and the Williamson is favored by local anglers.

Normally July and early August produce prime fishing throughout the Williamson as the big fish move upriver from Klamath Lake. Sometime in August the fishing falls off in the main river, but continues to improve upstream well into September as the fish move up to spawn.

We fished almost exclusively with leech patterns on fast-sinking lines during my July trip, but these were used because so few trout had moved upriver during the poor water conditions. Actually, the Williamson is rich in both insect life and other edibles for its large trout. In addition to leeches, sculpins, baby mullet and short-nosed suckers, there are abundant mayfly, stonefly, midge and caddis hatches. Caddis are especially abundant. One evening while fishing the wadable water upstream from the Chiloquin Bridge, the bottom was so encrusted with caddis cases it crunched underfoot. According to Chad Carroll, the hatch of the giant October Caddis *Dicosmoecus* can produce spectacular fishing to both the adult and the emerging pupae.

During my July trip, the big *Hexagenia* mayflies were just beginning their evening emergence, and would normally have produced outstanding dry-fly fishing. In fact, the *Hex* hatch was one of the prime reasons for the timing of my trip. However, due to the scarcity of fish in the river because of the poor water conditions, I saw only a few sporadic rises.

It was frustrating to sit in our quietly drifting boat and watch the huge cream-colored duns sail by unmolested. Occasionally, a heavy splash could be heard somewhere off in the growing darkness and the hair on the back of my neck would stand on end. One could only fantasize about the fishing that must take place in a normal year when the large 'bows are gorging themselves on the big mayflies.

Originally, the Williamson flowed through the Klamath Indian Reservation, and until the late fifties the river produced many large trout. With the opening of the water to the public, however, bait fishing and liberal bag limits soon took their toll. As fishermen carried out long stringers full of large fish, the quality of the fishing began to deteriorate.

Finally a group of anglers headed by Polly Rosborough and Dick Winters decided that something had to be done to save the once magnificent river, and they organized the Klamath Country Fly Casters. The group set the guidelines for the fight to save the river by preventing overkill. It encouraged other groups to join it and carried the battle to the state capitol in Salem.

Eventually the group's efforts paid off and bag limits were reduced. With this success the Klamath Country Fly Casters went on to promote public education concerning catch-and-release fishing, assisted with rebuilding the river's spawning areas, helped the State Game Commission with fish tagging operations and angler surveys, and began Vibert box experiments to help restore brown trout to certain areas of the river.

Today, thanks to the efforts of this dedicated group, the numbers and average size of Williamson trout have increased markedly and the river is regaining its former glory.

Current Williamson regulations permit fishing by any legal method between Spring Creek and the Chiloquin Bridge, but anglers floating the river must get out of the boat to fish. Between the Chiloquin Bridge and Oregon Highway 97 angling is permitted from boats, and fish may be taken by artificial flies and lures only. The legal limit on the entire river is two trout a day over twelve inches long. Since regulations sometimes change, visiting anglers should check the current regs before fishing.

Both browns and rainbows inhabit the Williamson and its tributaries, but roughly 90 percent of the fish are rainbows. While they exist higher up in the river, the biggest browns are found below Collier Park where Spring Creek enters the main river. The angler seeking the big browns would do well to concentrate on the Beatty area of the Sprague River where fish in the four- to nine-pound class will be found with some regularity.

But it's the big rainbow that have given the Williamson its reputation, and the word big should not be taken lightly. During a typical year, the rainbows will average four to seven pounds, and the largest trout that Richard Henry has taken on flies have been in the fourteen to fifteen pound class. He and Randy take great pleasure in telling of the day they landed and released over thirty fish up to twelve pounds on size 12 caddis pupae. It's such fishing that puts the Williamson River in a class by itself.

Anglers visiting the Chiloquin area to fish the Williamson and its tributaries, the Sprague River and Spring Creek, should be aware that accommodations are scarce in the immediate area.

The Rapids Motel on Highway 97 at Chiloquin has provided Spartan motel accommodations, and meals can be obtained next door at the truck stop. Another alternative is to find a motel room in Klamath Falls about 25 miles south of Chiloquin.

The lone bright spot — and that is very bright — has been found at Take It Easy Ranch, located about ten miles northwest of Chiloquin on Highway 62 just outside of Fort Klamath.

Take It Easy Ranch is a first-class fishing lodge operated by Cynthia and Randy Sparacino, and it's a fly-fishing-only operation. The ranch offers beautiful cabins, excellent food, a well-stocked fly shop, library, fly-tying facilities, and other amenities for the comfort and convenience of fly fishers and their families.

The delightful accommodations are only part of the attraction, though. The ranch also contains two superb private spring creeks, Squaw Creek and Fort Creek, that are reserved for guests only. Both streams are so clear that gin would look off-color by comparison. They have abundant hatches and a bountiful supply of trout in the two- to four-pound class. Angling is barbless hook, catch-and-release only.

Another spring creek, the Wood River, provides additional fly-fishing just a few miles up the road. At its headwaters, the Wood bubbles from the ground, forming a pool that looks exactly like

Yellowstone's Morning Glory Pool — except that this one is many, many times larger. After emerging from the pool, the Wood meanders through the lush countryside with an abundance of undercut banks, log jams, quiet pools and challenging fishing. Delightful.

Anglers who like to camp will find a little-known primitive camping area, the Jackson F. Kimball State Park, right on the banks of Morning Glory Pool. It's hard to imagine a prettier spot to camp, and when I was there in July, I found only one tent site occupied.

Finally, no trip to the area would be complete without taking the thirty minute drive up to Crater Lake National Park. It's a beautiful place, well worth missing a half day's fishing to see.

For more information contact Take It Easy Ranch, P. O. Box 408, Fort Klamath, OR 97526, (503) 381-2328. Overnight guests have been accommodated on a "space available" basis, and reservations have been accepted for a stay of two nights or longer.

8.

The Land of
the Midnight Sun

The Northwest Territories of Canada perch like a crown atop the North American Continent. Their vastness almost defies the imagination as they stretch more than 2,000 miles from east to west, and 1,700 miles from the sixtieth parallel to the North Pole encompassing an area of more than 1.3 million square miles. And it's a jewel encrusted crown, as thousands upon thousands of deep blue lakes sparkle across its breadth like so many priceless sapphires.

Not surprisingly, many of the lakes and rivers in this pristine wilderness are filled with trophy sized lake trout, charr, grayling, and northern pike, and for many anglers the Northwest Territories have become a Mecca — a land to dream of for that once-in-a-lifetime fishing trip. But that's the paradox, since most *fly* fishermen rarely think of the Northwest Territories at all. This really isn't fly fishing water — or so the story goes.

In fact, while considering the possibility of doing a Great Waters section on the Northwest Territories for *Fly Fisherman*, we weren't even certain that the area deserved such a classification in view of our readers' tastes. But still — there was all of this water and all of those *big* fish in that exotic land. There seemed to be only one answer: I had to go there and look it over for myself.

Frankly, my research trip did not get off to a very auspicious beginning. After struggling to stack my heap of fishing and camera gear onto his cart, the bellhop in my hotel in Yellowknife began to extoll the wonders of the fishing I would experience during my stay. My already elevated spirits took another leap higher, but the mood was short-lived.

For at the first mention of the words "fly rod," the porter looked incredulous. Taken aback for only a moment, he said, very matter of factly, "You might as well go home right now. You won't catch a fish."

I must have looked shocked, for he continued, "No, I'm serious. Fish up here won't take flies."

I argued a bit, and tried to convince him that fish are only fish and if they could be taken by anything, they could probably be taken on a fly, but he couldn't be swayed. "You might as well go home," he muttered again as he trudged off down the hallway.

Fortunately, the bellhop proved to be wrong or you wouldn't be reading this, but I discovered that his attitude was quite common among the residents of the Northwest Territories. Most of them had never seen a fly fisherman, and many were certain that I would be wasting my time to fish with such tackle.

On the other hand, I found the lodge owners where I visited most receptive to my desires to fish with flies, and they were very much interested in discovering how well I would do with the long rods. Without exception, the owners took great care to provide me with guides who were willing to work with me in my experiments and who were interested in learning about fly fishing.

The latter is an important point, since some of the native guides are primarily interested in catching lots of big fish, and they may feel handicapped when guiding fly fishermen. It is entirely possible that you could encounter antagonistic guides, and while I didn't see it, I did hear stories of guides or lodge owners who flatly didn't like fly fishing.

Therefore, before booking a trip to any lodge in the Northwest Territories, be certain that the owner knows that you intend to fish with flies, and that he will provide guides who are willing to work with you. This should be made absolutely clear before you go to avoid potential problems.

The fishing reputation of the Northwest Territories has been built primarily upon large lake trout — fish in the twenty- to forty-pound range are relatively common, those of over fifty pounds are possible, and almost every cast has the potential of hooking a new world record. However, since lake trout are generally considered to be deep water fish, they are usually thought to be unsuited for pursuit with fly tackle.

Fortunately, this is only partly true. Many of the lakes in the Northwest Territories are so cold that the big trout don't have to go deep to find the temperature they normally prefer, and they can often be located well within the range of the fly fisherman.

In addition to lake trout, northern pike inhabit most of the waters of the Northwest Territories, and it is probably safe to say that the best angling in the world for these voracious predators is found here. Primarily fish of the shallow, weedy bays and backwaters, the pike are prime targets for fly fishermen. Most pike fishing can be done with a bass type popping bug on a floating line, and the smashing strike of a twenty pounder can leave the most jaded angler weak in the knees.

Grayling, Arctic charr, whitefish, walleye and inconnu (sheefish) round out the fly fishing spectrum in the Northwest Territories, and each is available in record sizes.

The excellent fishing is only a part of the Northwest Territories story, though. The rest of it is found in the country itself. The entire experience of the north country is unique, and it's an experience that makes the history and geography books come alive. The words "Arctic Circle," "the midnight sun," "eskimo," and "tundra" become real and take on new meanings as you travel across this vast, untamed land by

Fly fishing for Arctic charr in the Northwest Territories of Canada—
"The Land of the Midnight Sun."

plane and boat. Just being there is exciting.

Still, it is possible that fly fishing in the Northwest Territories will not appeal to all fly fishermen. If your idea of the ultimate fly fishing challenge is light tackle angling for spooky brown trout in a spring creek, and you would prefer not to indulge in "coarse" fishing, the trip may not be for you.

On the other hand, few fly fishermen will ever have the opportunity to routinely take fish that weigh in double figures, and to do it literally until their arms ache. This opportunity, combined with the "total arctic experience," just might make the Northwest Territories the perfect spot for your trip-of-a-lifetime. And if you happen to be primarily a bass and panfish angler, the fly fishing in the Land of the Midnight Sun will suit your style perfectly. You'll think you've found paradise!

The Northwest Territories are divided into two rather distinct climactic zones, the Arctic and the sub-Arctic, and the weather and fishing seasons will vary depending upon exactly where you are in this vast area. In the southern portions of the Territories, the fishing will be good from two to three weeks after ice-out in mid-May until ice-up in October, while in the northern areas closer to the Arctic Circle, the season is much shorter — from July through September. Lodges in the area will suggest the best times for your visit.

During the summer months, anglers can expect a wide variety of weather conditions ranging from warm, sunny days in the mid-seventies to cold, rainy days in the thirties, and the nights are generally cool enough to make a sweater or light jacket feel comfortable. Through most of the summer months there will be from twenty to twenty-four hours of daylight depending upon your proximity to the Arctic Circle.

You should also be prepared for local weather phenomena produced by the very cold water in some of the northern lakes such as Great Bear. For example, you may be comfortably warm in camp with the air temperature in the seventies. When you travel many miles in an open boat to your fishing destination, however, the air over the extremely cold water will be considerably colder. The wind chill produced by the moving boat will reduce the effective temperature even further, and you'll find it necessary to wear heavy sweaters, jackets, caps, gloves and windbreakers to keep warm.

Thus, no matter what time of the summer you visit the Northwest Territories, your clothing should be adequate for a wide range of conditions. And don't forget your rain gear.

An absolute must for anyone planning to visit the Northwest Territories is *The Explorer's Guide to Canada's Arctic* available at no charge from Travel Arctic, Yellowknife, Northwest Territories, Canada X1A 2L9. If you are even dreaming of the remote possibility of a trip to the area, be sure to write for this comprehensive guide. It contains virtually everything you'll ever want to know about travel, lodging, and fishing in the Northwest Territories.

Great Slave Lake

Located some 550 miles north of Edmonton, Great Slave Lake covers a surface area of more than ten thousand square miles, and along with Great Bear Lake, provides the major fishery of the region. Visiting anglers will usually gain access to the lake either through the city of Yellowknife or Hay River, both of which are served by highways and airlines.

With such a vast watershed available, the most practical arrangement is to make reservations at one of the many fine lodges situated on the lake. Since most of these cannot be reached by road, chartered float plane service is usually provided from either Yellowknife or Hay River.

Fly fishing for lake trout in Great Slave proved to be either relatively easy or difficult depending upon exactly where it was done. I found it to be quite difficult to take fish on flies in the main lake, since the fish tended to be spread out and harder to locate. Under such conditions, trolling a large spoon on spinning or casting gear would cover more water and produce more fish, and the angler who is not a "purist" would do well to try such tactics. Trolling a streamer on extra fast sinking fly line would also produce in the open water, but such a technique cannot strictly be called "fly fishing."

A better bet for the fly fisherman is to have the guide take you to smaller bays and channels where the trout will be concentrated in shallow water. Under such conditions, fly casting from the boat or wading will be extremely effective. In fact, it is quite likely that you will out-produce the spin fishermen under such conditions.

I found just such a situation in the Stark River which flows out of Great Slave Lake within walking distance of my lodge. I would often go to the river after dinner and wade along several sand bars while casting streamers on sinking tip lines. Without exception, I consistently caught more lakers in the six- to twelve-pound range than the spin fishermen by a wide margin — much to their consternation.

My most effective streamers were tied to imitate smolts or small baitfish, and had a tubular body of silver mylar piping with a wing of white, blue and purple, or white, blue and green FisHair. The flies were about three inches in length, and could be cast easily with a number eight line. While fishing in the open water of the main lake, I found similar streamers of up to six inches in length ahead of a very fast sinking 10-weight shooting head to be more effective. Tippets testing 8 to 10 pounds are adequate for the smaller fish, and 12 to 15 pound should be used with the larger flies.

Though lake trout are the "glamour fish" of the region, the giant northern pike or "jackfish" may provide the most excitement for the fly fisherman. My first experience with the Arctic pike came during my first day when Stan, a Chipewyan Indian guide from Jerry Bricker's Frontier Fishing Lodge where I was staying, took me to "The Gap" — a long, weed filled area of Stark Lake that is connected to Great Slave by the Stark River.

Stan, not at all convinced that pike could be taken on flies, rolled his eyes skyward when I tied a large clipped deer hair mouse tied on a 5/0 hook to my floating 10-weight line, but, typically, he didn't say a word. My first cast dropped the mouse about seventy feet away near the edge of a large weed bed, and I hadn't stripped it back more than ten feet when the mouse was engulfed by a very large pike.

Stan let out a very uncharacteristic "whoop," and watched in sheer amazement as the big fish thrashed and tailwalked all around the boat before finally being brought to net. It weighed slightly over fifteen pounds, and Stan became a believer on the spot.

That first pike was followed by many more, and in the days to come I again found the fly rod to be even more effective than casting or spinning gear for taking these voracious fish. Large streamers (red and white, or yellow) also produced pike, but the large deer hair mice on floating lines were by far my favorites since they provided the added excitement of the often explosive surface take. And watching a large pike chase the swimming mouse always created almost unbearable anticipation and shouts of, "Here he comes!" My largest pike weighed something over eighteen pounds, but there are many well in excess of twenty pounds just waiting to be caught.

Whether using surface bugs or hair streamers, it is important to use a short section of shock tippet next to the fly when casting to the needle-toothed northern pike. After trying a variety of shock tippets including nylon coated wire, I determined that about ten inches of ordinary monofilament testing at least sixty pounds worked best. Occasionally even this would be inadequate, and a fish would slice through the leader like a razor blade, but in general it worked fine.

Be sure to check the tippet for nicks after each fish and replace it when you feel any roughness. You'll need a good supply of deer hair mice and bass bugs to replace those lost to the savage fish during a week's fishing, and a long-nosed pliers is essential to keep your fingers away from the toothy jaws while disengaging the fly. Fingers and pike teeth definitely do not mix.

In addition to the lake trout and pike of the Great Slave area, large grayling often provided excellent sport on a 4-6 weight outfit. Almost any small flies — dries and nymphs from size 12 to 18 — would produce when I found feeding fish. At times the water's surface was covered with the spreading rings of rising grayling and the action was extremely fast.

To call my expedition to Great Slave Lake a success is an understatement of the first magnitude. I proved to my satisfaction and to the amazement of the "locals" that fly fishing was unquestionably an effective method for taking the big fish of the Arctic. I could hardly wait to get back to Yellowknife and tell my bellhop of my success. Unfortunately, when I returned it was his day off, and he never heard the story. I imagine to this day he's going around telling people, "Fish up here won't take flies!"

Mackenzie River

It is not surprising that a land that contains two gigantic lakes such as Great Bear and Great Slave should also hold a river of prodigious proportions, and the mighty Mackenzie fills the bill nicely. One of the world's largest rivers, the Mackenzie is several miles wide at its headwaters where it emerges from the southwest end of Great Slave Lake to begin its twelve-hundred-mile journey to the Arctic Ocean. Along the way, it drains about one-fifth of all of Canada's waters, and provides a major transportation lane for goods being shipped to the wilderness communities of the north.

It is also safe to say that the upper Mackenzie River provides some of the world's best fly fishing for northern pike. While the river is very wide at its source, it is extremely shallow outside of the navigation channel, and its myriad of islands are surrounded by broad, weedy flats that are home to unbelievable numbers of outsized pike.

As in the rest of the Northwest Territories, most anglers on the Mackenzie are not fly fishermen, but the fly rod should be the method of choice. A fly rod with a floating 9-10 weight line and a floating deer hair mouse or large weedless bass bug is without a doubt the most efficient tool for catching pike in these shallow, weedy waters. In one instance, by actual count, two of us fishing with fly tackle out-fished ten other anglers by nearly ten to one. In several hours of fishing we accounted for approximately sixty pike averaging around seven to eight pounds and going to approximately fifteen pounds. Fish to over twenty pounds are possible on any cast.

In fact, the fishing is so good that the average length of stay at the Brabant Lodge where I stayed was reported to be four days rather than the more traditional week. The reason? The guests just plain get fished out. Now that's good fishing!

Another interesting quarry in the Mackenzie River are the whitefish. Not to be confused with the more familiar Rocky Mountain whitefish, the lake whitefish of the Arctic are heavy fish, strong fighters, and a real challenge to take on small flies and light tackle. The fish will run to well over three pounds, and their strength combined with their paper thin mouths make them quite difficult to catch.

While I had only limited experience with the whitefish, I found that small dark nymphs (size 12 to 16) and small dries in the same sizes would produce once the fish were located. A knowledgeable guide is almost essential in finding these cruising fish, and once found, caution is needed to approach them in the clear water of the Mackenzie.

Great Bear Lake

The fly fishing on Great Bear Lake proved to be quite similar to that on Great Slave Lake, and my best success with lake trout was found in the channels and smaller bays where the fish tended to be more concentrated. The northern pike were just as big and abundant and eager to eat deer hair mice in the weed filled back water areas as they had been on Great Slave. And I just may have released what might have been a new world record grayling — and realized it an instant too late.

During my visit to Great Bear Lake, I stayed at Branson's Lodge. Ernie Dolansky, the manager, flies a float-equipped Cessna which greatly increased our fishing range. In addition to the main lodge, Branson's runs an outpost tent camp well above the Arctic Circle, and guests often fly out for an overnight stay and fishing.

Another highlight was the day we flew a couple of hundred miles north of the Arctic Circle to a river near the Coronation Gulf of the Arctic Ocean to fish for charr. These powerful fish were just in from the salt and weighed about twelve to sixteen pounds. In the fast, deep water the river we were fishing, they proved to be a a real challenge for our fly tackle.

A visit to the far north is an incredible experience. During my stay I saw bears, wolves and caribou, and more ptarmigan, ducks and geese than I could count. And a walk across the top of the world on tundra that is covered by a million dwarfed flowers of every conceivable color is never to be forgotten.

The quality of the fly fishing available in the Northwest Territories depends entirely upon your own mental attitude. Big water, heavy tackle and long boat rides may not appeal to you. But as they say, "If you ain't tried it, don't knock it." If you are searching for new experiences, huge fish and the excitement of new challenges, you will find them in abundance in the Land of the Midnight Sun — the Northwest Territories of Canada.

9.

Parents, Kids, And Fly Rods

This article, first published in July, 1979 Fly Fisherman, *was the First Place winner of the Buck Knives Outdoor Writing Award competition at the 1980 Outdoor Writers of America national convention.*

Eric was only seven years old, but his grin was almost as long as the small rainbow trout that wriggled in his hand. It was his first fish on a fly rod, and he had also tied the small, brown-hackled wet fly. He had a right to be proud. But he couldn't have been more proud at that moment than I was after watching him cast his fly and hook and land that fish. It wasn't large; it was just barely of legal length, but the first trout on a fly is a very important fish.

And although that moment was brief, it, too, was very important, for that moment marked both an end and a beginning. It was the end of a long period of waiting for a small boy, and the beginning of his education as a fly fisher.

I suppose almost every parent who fishes with the fly looks forward to sharing the joys of the sport with his or her children. We stare in wonder at the wiggling bundle in the crib and envision our beautiful little daughter laying out her first perfect cast, or our son tying his first perfect fly, and we wait for that day. For some the day comes easily, for some it comes with great difficulty, and for some it comes not at all.

Teaching your own child to fish would seem to be a very simple and natural thing. It's no big deal: "Come on, son. Let's go fishin'." But don't be misled! Whether or not you end up with a lifelong fishing partner may well depend upon how you respond to the innocent question, "Daddy, will you teach me how to fly-fish?"

While the question may be innocent, it is significant because it indicates that the child has an interest in learning the sport. Normally, of course, this is no problem — kids love to fish. But occasionally an over-anxious parent will attempt to push a child into the activity before the desire is there, and this is almost guaranteed to cause problems. When pushed, the child will be a difficult student at best, and at worst he'll be completely turned off by the whole thing.

A better approach is to relax and let nature take its course. The exposure that your child has to the sport as you tinker with your tackle, tie flies and practice casting on the lawn should eventually pique his natural curiosity, and he'll probably be eager to try it. So — the first rule is: Don't push the subject, but wait until the interest is there.

This interest may pop up at almost any age, and typically it shows up while the child is still too young to really become a proficient fly fisherman. The young muscles simply do not have adequate strength or coordination for handling a fly rod, and the child lacks the necessary mental discipline to be taught the needed skills.

This leads to the next rule: The child must be physically ready to learn the sport. Unfortunately, there is no set age at which this readiness will occur. Some will be ready at five or six years of age, while others may be well into their teens before they have both the interest and the physical readiness. However, it's easy to tell when this stage is reached. The child will tell you. Or more correctly, he'll show you. I suppose my boys were about four when they first asked to try to cast as I was practicing on the lawn one day. Of course, I let them try it after a quick run-through of the basic points of a simple short cast. It didn't take more than five minutes, however, to show that they simply could not handle the long rod. Sporadically over the next couple of years the whole thing was repeated.

Finally, in rather discouraged tones, Eric asked, "When will I ever be able to do it?" I replied, "When you're ready, you'll know it. We'll try again another time."

Then one day when he was seven, it happened. After the now-familiar initial instructions, Eric stopped the rod on his backcast, paused, brought the rod forward and stopped again. Twenty-five feet of line straightened and fell to the ground in front of him. He looked up at me and beamed.

By coincidence, his younger brother, Jeff, was also seven years old when that eventful day occurred for him. As any parent knows, though, brothers and sisters are likely to be as different as night and day in almost every respect. Don't expect them all to be ready at the same age, or you may be disappointed.

Until the interest and the physical readiness coincide, it is important to feed and nurture the interest without allowing the child to become discouraged. They love to "help" Dad or Mom re-spool fly lines, sort hooks, clean tackle and do all sorts of small tasks, and such activities should certainly be encouraged. It'll be fun for both of you, and it will go a long way toward maintaining the interest that's so important.

Once it becomes apparent that the child is ready to begin fly-fishing in earnest, it is necessary to give adequate consideration to the tackle that will be used. For most kids, a modern, lightweight fiberglass rod, 7½ feet long and designed for a 6-weight line will be ideal. Small hands and underdeveloped muscles need lightweight tackle. On the other hand, the precise timing required by rods of less than seven feet make them generally unsuitable for neophyte casters.

And don't make the common mistake of expecting the child to learn with old discarded tackle and mismatched line. "Dad's old junk" has probably discouraged more kids (and wives, too) from learning the sport than any other single cause. If you can't use the tackle yourself, you really can't expect a beginner to learn with it. Another rule: The beginner's tackle should be properly balanced and of appropriate size.

Whenever possible, children should be given their own tackle. Pride of ownership will help them learn to care for it and will go a long way toward maintaining interest in the sport over the difficult early days. Perhaps the very best way to provide a suitable rod, and also the most economical, is to assemble one from a kit as a joint project. The assembly is very easy even if you've never attempted it before, and the value of such a venture is almost immeasurable. Regardless of the quality of the finished product, it will remain a treasure for a lifetime.

The child can, of course, begin to learn to cast with one of your rods before he actually has one of his own, and such instruction should occur well before your first actual fishing trip. There will simply be too many new things to learn the first time on the water to expect the child to learn to cast, too! So—the next rule is: Teach them some basic casting before you take them fishing.

Initial casting sessions on the grass or a pond should be short and fun. Children have limited attention spans, and they tire both mentally and physically rather quickly. The practice should never continue until they lose interest. It's better to leave them begging for more than wishing the whole thing would end so they could do something else.

Remember, too, that children learn best by imitation; that is, by watching and doing, rather than by long, involved, technical explanations. A discussion of casting arcs, tip speed, power application and so on could as well be given in a foreign language for all the good it will do most children. The majority of children's instructors talk too much. Take your rod along and show them what to do.

Even the simplest cast is made up of many components, and it is usually a mistake to try to emphasize all of these at one time. A beginner cannot mentally concentrate upon the grip, the wrist, the backcast, the pause, the forward cast, the turnover and the stop simultaneously. Therefore, after the child has been given a general introduction to casting, it is best to concentrate on only one component at a time. For example, have the child do a complete cast, but concentrate only on the stop at the end of the backcast. Don't worry if the rest of the cast isn't exactly right—just emphasize the stop. Then, as that particular component becomes a fixed habit, start to concentrate on another aspect of the cast.

If it's convenient, a little practice every day is preferable to a long session at wide intervals. Twenty minutes a day, for example, is much better than an hour of practice every three days. The short practice periods prevent fatigue and maintain the child's interest, and they make it very convenient to emphasize only a single casting component each day. "Yesterday we concentrated on stopping the rod on the backcast. Today let's work on stopping it on the forward cast."

Such a teaching technique will help to insure that each component will become an ingrained habit before you move on to the next, and it will also prevent you from moving too quickly. If you try to progress too rapidly, the child's mental circuits will soon overload, then he won't be able to remember everything that's supposed to be done. The rule, then, is let one thing become a habit before moving on to the next.

Of course you shouldn't expect children to be polished performers with the long rod before they go fishing, but they should have mastered a few simple things. They should be able to perform a basic cast of twenty-five or thirty feet with reasonably good form, and they should know how to retrieve and extend line. After that, it's time to catch a fish!

When taking the first fishing trip, there must be one primary consideration — do whatever you can to guarantee that the kids will catch fish! Take them to an easy stream, let them catch little, stocked fish, or go bluegill fishing, but if at all possible make sure they're successful. Nothing generates excitement like a fish on the end of the line, and nothing produces disinterest and boredom more quickly than a long day with no action.

For example, all kids seem to love worm fishing. There's tremendous excitement in watching a colorful bobber dance and twitch as a small fish plays with the worm and kids squeal with delight as the bobber dives out of sight. Even the anticipation is fun as they wait for the quiet bobber to make its first wiggle. Worm fishing is exciting! And if we expect to interest the kids in fly-fishing, this same excitement has to be present. Take them where they'll catch some fish — any kind of fish!

To avoid frustrations, make the fishing as simple as possible. This will usually mean wet-fly or streamer fishing with a floating line, simple across and down-stream casting, and stripped retrieves. Take them where there are fish and they can't miss. Yes, even if you're a dry-fly purist, let them try it wet the first few times. This is an investment in the future, and they have to be successful.

The first days on the water can be trying times for both the child and the parent. Flies will snag in trees, lines will tangle, strikes will be missed, and tempers will flare. But remember, this is supposed to be fun. Don't expect or demand too much too soon. Laugh a lot and don't dwell on the mistakes that are certain to be made. Instead, give lots of encouragement by complimenting the good things the child does. Constant harping on the problems is guaranteed to produce discouragement.

I'll have to bite my tongue as I say it, but don't get angry with the child no matter what happens. This is a tough one, and I've blown it myself more than once by getting upset at little irritations when I was trying to teach my boys to fly-fish. I suppose it happens when we lose perspective of what it is we're trying to do, but such anger only leads to further frustrations for a child who is really trying very hard to catch a fish.

I can vividly recall one fine afternoon when I was fishing alone on a very difficult Western spring creek and was having relatively little success. I was sitting on the bank pondering my next move when my ears were assaulted by an angry shout from somewhere below me.

"No, damn it! I said put it next to the bank, not two feet out!" A moment of silence followed, then, "You can't slap the fly down! You'll scare the fish!" Then it grew even louder: "How the hell do you expect to catch any fish if you won't do what I tell you, damn it!"

The harangue continued for at least half an hour, as I sat there feeling very sorry for the hapless student. I couldn't see the father and son just around the bend, but the lad had my sympathy. I don't know if he ever became a fly fisherman. I hope so, but I'm sure it wasn't an easy process if he did.

Unfortunately, teaching anything to members of your own family is often more difficult than teaching strangers. I like to think that I'm a pretty good teacher. In fact, that's my profession. But I know that I don't teach nearly as well when I'm trying to teach something to a member of my own family.

In the first place, I don't have the patience I'd have with someone from outside the family. I suppose that I take short cuts, expect faster results and am much more critical than I'd be with a stranger. At the same time, the family members, whether it's my wife or one of the boys, don't respond to my teaching in the same manner they would to another instructor. It's too easy for them to disagree, argue, or say no to me. Possibly they'd try a little harder for a stranger.

This, of course, is not to discourage you from attempting to teach your own children to fly-fish; it is merely to make you aware of some of the problems that may arise. If you're alert to the potential problems, you may be able to head them off before they occur.

I imagine it's too much to expect that we all could teach the members of our own families as though they were strangers, but that is a clue as to how to solve an occasional sticky problem. Swap kids for a day on the stream. I have had a number of opportunities to take the children of various friends for a day of fishing instruction on the water, and without exception, we've always had a great day. So if you find your instructional situation breaking down sometime, find a friend with the same problem and trade kids. It'll do you all good.

This also points up the advantage of enrolling your children in an organized fly-fishing class, if one is available in your community. Many Trout Unlimited chapters or Federation of Fly Fishers groups or other local clubs, as well as YMCA's, high schools and colleges, camps or commercial fly-fishing schools, offer excellent opportunities for children to learn the art of fly-fishing. Or, if such a class doesn't exist in your area, one can easily be formed by a group of interested parents. You don't have to be experts at the sport in order to provide a very good learning experience for your children.

The first few times you take your children on a fishing expedition, it should be a trip for *them*. Keep in mind that the purpose of the trip is to help them learn to fish. All too often, the child is deposited on a handy sandbar or riffle and told to fish while Dad goes off in search of his own sport. Left to his own devices, the child will quickly tire of the whole affair, and the event will degenerate into one of frustration for all. Far better to forget about your own fishing and concentrate on teaching. It will pay many dividends in the long run.

Of course, a fishing trip should not become merely one long fishing lesson. There's more to being on the stream than simply fishing. When you stop to think about it, I'm sure you'll find that some of your most memorable fishing trips involved a great many experiences that really had very little to do with the actual fishing. If you expect your children to develop a love for the sport, there must be plenty of opportunity for them to share in the whole spectrum of events that create a successful fishing trip. In the words of a popular song, "You've got to stop and smell the roses."

"Smelling the roses" can take many forms, aside from its literal meaning. Insects, clouds and so many other things all deserve to be admired. The sound of bubbling water is new music to be enjoyed, and just sitting on a rock talking is a pleasure that many children and parents never have.

My youngest son, Jeff, still talks about "our" day on a small feeder stream of the Smith River in Montana. Jeff was ten at the time, and he was already a pretty fair fly fisherman. We'd spent the morning hopscotching up the little stream taking turns at its small pools and dancing riffles, and the fishing had been very good. The day had grown hot in the narrow canyon, and as Jeff lay on his belly for a cool drink of stream water following our noon lunch he said, "Boy, it sure would be great to go for a swim!"

He didn't have to convince me, and I replied, "Let's do it."

"Do you mean it?"

"I sure do!" I said, pulling off my hot chest waders.

We didn't spend much time skinny-dipping in the icy water, but neither of us will ever forget that day.

Nor will we ever forget the day in late August two years later when I took Jeff on his first float trip down the Henry's Fork in southern Idaho. Jeff had long anticipated the trip after hearing many of my tales of the river over the years, and we were both excited as we pushed the canoe out into the smooth water. The hoards of early-summer anglers were gone from the river. It was completely deserted, and we saw no one else for the entire day.

Unfortunately, as so often happens when sharing a river with someone for the first time, the fishing did not live up to expectations. Due to water release from the dam, the river was high and completely out of shape. It was one of the few times that I had ever seen the water discolored to that degree. Although a few mayflies came off the water throughout the day, we saw no rises.

We fished for hours without success. Changing flies, tactics, or our location on the river made no difference. Finally, in mid-afternoon, a very small rainbow managed to attach itself to my fly, and it was to be our only fish. Jeff cast until his arm ached and he could barely grip the rod, but he caught nothing.

It sounds like a rather grim day, doesn't it? It wasn't. For as we sat on the bank of a small island, Jeff was able for the first time to watch a belted kingfisher diving into the water for food. We watched eagles soar in the bright blue sky, and we saw dozens of ducks and sandhill cranes. We watched long-billed curlews strut through the streamside grass and mayflies struggle in the water to free themselves of their nymphal cases.

As our canoe slid around a bend of the river, we both gasped when we saw a trumpeter swan swimming near the bank. We stopped paddling and the canoe drifted closer until the swan spread its wings and lifted into the air. Its wing beats hitting the water resounded like gunshots as the giant bird ran along the surface trying to gain flight speed. And we sat in awe.

Farther down the river we both laughed and hollered as the canoe rushed through the boiling water of the last riffle and into the still water below. We were quiet then, too. It had been a long day with no fish, and we were tired. The silence was broken when the canoe scraped to a stop on the gravel bar above the Osborn Bridge; then it was quiet again.

Finally Jeff spoke, "Gee, that was a great day, Dad!" I knew then that the family had another fly fisherman.

Yes, we teach them many things besides how to catch fish when we take our children fishing. They learn our philosophy and our attitudes about nature, conservation, streamside etiquette, other people and life itself. We may not even be fully aware that we are teaching these very important concepts. But we are. We teach them by our actions, which speak at least as loud as our words. In fact, it's quite likely that what we do and how we do it will be remembered after the words we have spoken are long forgotten.

The teaching of our children is an awesome responsibility and must not be taken too lightly. For in our children lies the future of clean air and water, wild fish, and the sport of fly-fishing.

10.

Unique Discoveries

A fishing writer's life has many pleasant moments, but one of the most rewarding events is the discovery of new angling waters. And when those new waters are found in an incredibly beautiful and unique setting, the discovery is especially exciting.

Though new discoveries are rare in these days when most prime angling waters are almost too well known, during the course of my travels around the western United States and Canada it has been my very good fortune to stumble across a number of very special fly fishing opportunities. I'd like to share them with you.

Hatheume Lake, British Columbia

There are numerous places in North America where one can find excellent stillwater trout fishing, but I know of nowhere else that it is accomplished in the manner found at the Hatheume Lake Resort in the Canadian province of British Columbia.

At first appearance the resort is no more unusual than any of hundreds of similar fishing camps across Canada and the United States. In fact, it looks like the archetypical wilderness resort. A large log lodge stands at the head of a row of snug log cabins, the breeze whispers through the thick pine forest, and the waves of the lake lap at the beach a few feet in front of each cabin. Beautiful, yes, but not unique.

The only indication that there is something special about the resort is the fleet of green Jeeps parked beside the main lodge. They can mean only one thing—there is someplace exciting to go in a four-wheel-drive vehicle. And that's the key to the uniqueness of the Hatheume Lake Resort. The resort offers the only access to a chain of eight lakes plus two others which have public access. These lakes, ranging in size from very small to quite large, are located entirely on private property, and are interconnected by a system of Jeep trails. They may be fished only by guests of the resort, and each cabin comes equipped with a Jeep in which to reach them.

Each lake is no more than twenty minutes or so from the lodge, and each has a small dock and a couple of wooden boats with outboard motors for use by the guests. In addition, a small storage shed at each lake contains seat cushions, extra fuel for the outboards, and landing nets.

All of the lakes contain the Kamloops strain of rainbow trout. These bright, rapidly growing fish are extremely strong, and when hooked, leap higher than any other rainbows that I've ever encountered. Their average size depends upon which lake is being fished, and the time of year — their growth rate is so rapid in these rich lakes that the fall fish will average considerably larger than those taken in the spring. When I fished the lakes in early July, the fish were averaging a chunky fourteen inches in length, and the largest taken was just shy of five pounds.

In some lakes, the fish are of smaller average size, but they are available in incredible numbers; in other lakes they run considerably larger, but there are fewer of them. Thus, you make the decision on which you prefer, and head for the appropriate lake. Since my wife was then a novice fly fisherman, I wanted to get her into a lot of action, so our first attempt was on little Rouse Lake which was reputed to be the place for a beginner. We weren't disappointed! On her first cast of the day using a dark black nymph as a tail fly and an olive nymph on a dropper, she caught two fat twelve inchers at the same time. By the end of the day we had both caught and released more fish than we could count.

This is another outstanding feature of the lodge — it is an excellent place for families. The fishing can be very challenging for the serious angler, as when the trout are delicately rising to drifting midge pupae, or it can be very easy and produce plenty of action for the neophyte. It would be a perfect place to teach children who are new to the sport.

With a few exceptions (June on Jerry Lake, for example) mayflies are not a major food source on these lakes, and caddis (sedge), midges, leeches, scuds, damsel flies, and dragonflies are more typical fare. Beginning with the lodge's opening on June 1, midges and caddis, along with some mayflies, provide the bulk of the action. Don't be misled by the name midges, though — pupal patterns which will be fished right in the surface film are tied on size 8-12 hooks, and are usually 3X long! Dark patterns seem to work best. Bucktail caddis patterns in burnt orange and brown (size 8-10) are also very effective.

Damsel and dragonfly nymphs become more significant in July and August, as do various scuds and fresh water "shrimp." And a long, slinky black marabou leech can be dynamite.

In September, Hatheume Lake itself has a tremendous hatch of Cinnamon Sedges (size 8) which, along with the ever present black midge pupae, produces some of the best fishing of the year for the fish which have been growing fat all summer. If you're looking for big fish, this is the prime time to find them.

The fine fly fishing is only a part of a trip to Hatheume, though. The rest of it is found when you stop your Jeep along a trail to watch a mother grouse scurry to hide her chicks under the fallen leaves, let a squirrel or Canadian jay eat from your hand, or watch an osprey soaring high above you in the deep blue sky. If you're lucky, as we were, you'll watch a pair of loons criss-cross in front of your boat while keeping their baby tucked out of sight behind one of them, as the other pulls the old "broken wing trick" to draw you away.

The "Hatheume experience" is very mellow, and not at all like the high pressure day-long fishing marathons sometimes encountered on fishing trips, and this is another facet which makes it an ideal vacation for the entire family. In fact, the resort has been owned and operated by two families, Tim and Janet Tullis and Gus and Leni Averill, and they have done their best to provide a comfortable, relaxed atmosphere. Customers are considered to be guests in their home, and by the end of the second day, everyone feels like one big family.

A typical day begins when juice and steaming coffee are brought to your cabin, followed by a breakfast of lumberjack proportions served family style in the main lodge. After a leisurely second cup of coffee, you pick up your lunch bag, hop into your Jeep, and head for your lake. And the term "your lake" is correct. Because these are private waters, you will have it all to yourself with no more than one other boat from the lodge to share it with. Many times you will be alone with your partner, the loons, and the ospreys. It's a delightful way to spend the day, and that's what helps to make this experience unique.

Most anglers fish until mid- to late afternoon, and return to camp in time for a shower and cocktails or coffee before dinner. If you've decided to keep any fish, Tim or Gus pick them up as they help you unload your Jeep, clean them, and either freeze or smoke them according to your instructions. Trophy fish for mounting are handled accordingly.

Following a magnificent home-cooked dinner, the most ardent anglers will take a boat from the main lodge to fish the evening midge hatch on Hatheume Lake, while the others curl up in front of the fireplace with a good book, a couple of friends or a backgammon board. Either way, it's a fitting end to a pleasant day.

The Hatheume Lake Resort is located near the town of Peachland, B.C., and is approximately 250 miles northwest of Spokane, Washington, 340 miles northeast of Seattle, or 55 miles northwest of Penticton, B.C. By car, the drive north along Highway 97 to Peachland is another highlight of the trip. The highway winds through the beautiful Okanogan Valley which is dotted with lush fruit orchards and Arabian horse ranches, and in season, fresh fruits are available from farm stands all along the road. During our trip in early July, we practically overdosed on freshly picked cherries — you can pick them yourself if you like — and if you haven't tasted fresh cherry cider, you really haven't lived.

The resort can also be reached by air via Pacific Western Airways from either Vancouver, B.C., or Calgary, Alberta. You can fly to Penticton and take a limousine to the resort, or you can fly to Kamloops, B.C., and arrange for a charter float plane direct to the lodge via either Central B.C. Air or Progress Air.

For further information contact Hatheume Lake Resort, P.O. Box 490, Peachland, B.C., Canada V0H 1X0.

K Bar L Ranch, Montana

The K Bar L Ranch is unique in every sense of the word, and it provides visiting anglers and their families with an exceptional Western experience.

Situated at the confluence of the north and the south forks of the North Fork of the Sun River, the K Bar L lies at an elevation of 4,800 feet on the eastern boundary of the famed Bob Marshall Wilderness Area. The setting is wild and remote, and even getting to the ranch is an adventure.

After leaving Interstate 15 near Wolf Creek south of Great Falls, you first drive approximately forty miles north on Montana State Highway 434 to the town of Augusta. A gravel road continues in a northwesterly direction for about twenty-eight miles from Augusta through the beautiful Sun River Canyon to the Gibson Dam.

The K Bar L has a "lower ranch" near the dam where you are met and transported to Gibson Lake and put aboard a jet boat for the trip to the headwaters of the reservoir. Finally, you climb onto a mule-drawn buckboard for the last leg of the journey. The scenery is spectacular during the entire trip, and as you approach the ranch it just keeps getting better.

Owned and operated by Nancy and Dick Klick, the K Bar L has been a family operated guest ranch catering to fishermen and hunters and their families for three generations.

Guests stay in snug log cabins, and excellent home cooked meals are served in the large log main lodge. Each cabin is heated by a small wood burning stove, and has running water available at an outside faucet. Centrally located buildings provide heated showers and toilet facilities.

An interesting feature of the ranch is the natural warm spring which supplies water to a large swimming pool, and, in addition, runs a turbine which generates electricity for lighting the ranch. While electric lighting is available twenty-four hours a day, the generated current is DC only, and appliances such as hair driers and electric razors cannot be used.

Though the comfort and genuine Western hospitality of the K Bar L are second to none, the real attraction of the ranch is the fishing. The sparkling clear waters of the north and south forks of the North Fork of the Sun River meet right at the ranch and offer many miles of outstanding fishing for cutthroat trout, rainbows, rainbow–cutthroat hybrids and Eastern brook trout. Fish in the ten- to fifteen-inch range are common, and some run as large as twenty inches.

Anglers can walk to either river from the ranch, but most fishermen will want to explore farther afield on horseback. Each guest is assigned to a horse for the duration of his or her stay, and many riding trails offer almost unlimited fishing opportunities within the Bob Marshall Wilderness Area. In fact, it's the riding that is the most unique feature of the ranch.

The Klicks take justifiable pride in their fine stable of well-mannered horses, and anglers with no previous riding experience need have no hesitancy in taking to the trail aboard a trusty steed. Novice riders are given instruction and guides along the trail. But the outstanding feature of the riding is that it is not typical "trail riding" in which the horse won't go unless there's a tail in front of his face. These are real Western horses, and anglers are encouraged to just get on and go.

I am anything but a horseman, but the experience of riding off alone over an incredibly beautiful mountain trail on a gentle, responsive horse was at least the equal of the excellent fishing that I found at the K Bar L. The fishing was all but forgotten as I admired the lofty peaks and lush mountain meadows filled with wild flowers, and counted deer, elk, big horn sheep and coyotes.

The fishing, though, was what brought me to the ranch, and I was not disappointed. I fished for four days and the only tracks I saw along the river were either my own or those of deer and elk. I saw no other anglers. During my first visit in late August, the rivers were low and clear, and though little insect life was in evidence, the fish responded very well to a floating caddis or 'hopper pattern, or a wet Muddler Minnow. I'm sorry to say that I cannot report on the numbers of fish taken — I lost count! I have since visited the K Bar L in both late June and July, and have found the conditions to be remarkably uniform during each visit.

Both rivers are of modest size, and can be well fished with a light 5-6 weight trout outfit. The rocky stream bottoms are clean and firm, and felt soled waders or hip boots provide adequate traction.

Due to heavy snow runoff, fly fishing at the K Bar L does not usually begin to be effective until about the first week of July in a normal year, but then it will be very good until the Klicks close to anglers around the first of September when they begin their hunting operation.

The K Bar L can accommodate up to thirty guests at a time, and it is possible to arrange a stay of any duration. In addition to the fishing, overnight or extended sightseeing horse pack trips into the Bob Marshall Wilderness Area are available, or the ranch can serve as a base of operations for backpacking.

Because of the versatility of its operation, the ranch is ideally suited to families made up of both anglers and non-anglers of all ages. Those who don't fish will have a great time riding and hiking, watching the abundant wildlife, taking pictures of the unsurpassed scenery, or just relaxing around the pool. The angler will be in his glory.

It is difficult to imagine a better all-around "Western experience" than is provided by the K Bar L Ranch. And the hospitality is genuine. One has the feeling that the Klicks are not serving customers, but are entertaining friends. And that is as it should be, for though you will arrive a stranger you will leave a friend.

For further information contact K Bar L Ranch, Augusta, Montana 59410. Winter and spring (406) 264-5806; summer and fall (406) 467-2771.
friends.

Seven Lakes Ranch, Colorado

A float tuber's paradise in the heart of Colorado is unexpected. Except for an occasional reservoir, Colorado is a land of tall peaks and rushing water; a land of skiing and stream fishing. But there is at least one remote spot in the Centennial State where the float tube reigns supreme—the 7-Lakes Ranch.

The 7-Lakes Ranch, located just outside of Meeker, Colorado, is nestled into an alpine valley at an elevation of 8,200 feet on the boundaries of the Whitewater National Forest and the Flattop Wilderness Area. A private guest ranch for anglers and their families, 7-Lakes is owned and operated by fly fishers Norm and Steb Sherwood, and as the name indicates, the ranch contains seven spring fed lakes—each with an abundance of trout.

Float tubers will find the little lakes to be just about perfect for their needs, and Norm has an air compressor available for inflating tubes. But, each lake also has canoes and aluminum boats available for guests who have not yet become initiated into the tubing fraternity.

Norm and Steb's philosophy is readily apparent in the way they run the ranch. As Norm says, "We wanted the type of resort where we would want to go ourselves. We wanted a family place, not a 'fishing camp,' but a place where families could come and have a good time whether everyone fished or not. We wanted a place that would suit the experienced fly fisher, but also a place where the kids could learn to fish, and where they would have a good opportunity to actually catch fish while they were learning."

The Sherwoods have succeeded very well in achieving their goal. Guests stay in comfortable, well appointed log cabins amid the pines and white trunked aspens at the edge of Cabin Lake, and they eat Steb's great homecooked meals in the large, log main lodge. Long before the end of the first day the feeling that you're a paying customer tends to disappear, and you feel as though you're just visiting old friends. The 7-Lakes is a that kind of place.

7-Lakes opens on Memorial Day, and the fishing is usually excellent. In fact, because these are spring fed lakes, they are little affected by snow runoff, and the ranch can provide very good fishing at a time when there is little available elsewhere due to high water.

The lakes contain lots of fresh water "shrimp" and fathead minnows, and early season fishing with small fluorescent green shrimp patterns (size 14-16) or weighted Muddlers is very good. Since there is no weed growth early in the season, sinking tip lines can be used effectively. The lakes contain brown, rainbow, cutthroat and brook trout, and the early season finds the browns and brookies, in particular, feeding voraciously.

In a normal year, surface activity begins near the end of June with the start of the mayfly hatches. A dry Hendrickson (size 14-16) is very effective at this time.

As soon as the weed growth starts around the edges of the lakes — say about the Fourth of July, the damsel fly provides about two weeks of the best fishing of the year. Interestingly, this is usually to the adults, although a nymph pattern can also be effective at this time, as well as a week or two before the adults are active. Norm's most successful pattern for matching the adult damsels consists of a slender olive green deer hair body, an upright, white calf tail wing, and a grizzly hackle tied parachute style.

With the start of the weed growth, floating lines become the most practical for all fishing.

Starting about the first of August, small Blue Duns (size 16-20) become effective matches for the naturals that are hatching.

Emergent midge patterns seem to be effective almost any time of year, as are size 12-14 Bitch Creek nymphs. These two patterns provided most of the fish caught during the time my son, Jeff, and I were at the ranch during the third week of July. I have no idea why the fish took the Bitch Creek so readily, but we tried it at Norm's suggestion, and it was a hot pattern.

According to Norm, the best time of the year may well be from September fifteenth until 7-Lakes closes at the end of October. The weather is beautiful, the fall colors magnificent, and the fish very cooperative.

Since the goal at 7-Lakes is to provide a quality fishing experience, the regulations are designed to maintain the fishing quality. Only single, barbless hooks and lures may be used, and though you may eat all the fish you want while at the ranch, only five fish may be taken home regardless of the length of your stay. Catch-and-release fishing is strongly encouraged.

In addition to the lake fishing, 7-Lakes offers very good stream fishing in the nearby White River after the water level drops about the twentieth of July (in a normal year). Three to five pound browns and rainbows, and a few cutts can be taken from the White, and the fishing progressively improves through the season and into October.

In the lakes, anglers can also expect to take some very fine fish. The largest cutthroat taken here was over five pounds, the biggest rainbow about eight pounds, and the largest brown over six pounds. During our stay, Jeff and I took many fish that were well over two pounds, and we broke off several that would have gone considerably larger.

The fishing is not the only attraction at 7-Lakes. There are almost unlimited opportunities for hiking, photography, sightseeing, wildlife observation, wild flower study and horse back riding. For those who desire to do so, an over night horse pack trip into the Wilderness Area or National Forest can even be arranged. Incidentally, the 7-Lakes

Ranch opens from Christmas through April for cross-country skiing, skating and other winter activities. Ski rentals, instruction and marked trails are available, and all cabins are winterized.

Steb enjoys taking guests for nature walks, and she is a wild flower expert who can assist with naming the many varieties of flowers you'll find in the lush high country meadows. If you like, she'll give you instruction on drying, pressing and preserving your special finds.

Norm provides excellent riding and horsemanship instruction for those who need it. We had the pleasure of watching him introduce a very small girl to the wonders of a very large horse, and his understanding, patience and knowledge were impressive. Equally important, the horses at 7-Lakes are extremely well mannered and gentle — a comforting fact for most fly fishers.

In addition to the fishing, a highlight of our trip to 7-Lakes was the day that Norm, Jeff, another guest and I rode into the high country. While climbing a ridge through the aspens, a huge bull elk with its antlers still in velvet rose out of the brush and watched us ride by. Wild flowers were everywhere, and as we rode along the height of land, the view of the rugged Colorado backcountry was incredible. It was a rare day.

The 7-Lakes Ranch has operated on the full American Plan, and the rates have been all inclusive with the exception of a river guide, if needed, and beer and wine. The minimum length of stay is two days, or three days on holiday weekends. With a ranch capacity of sixteen guests, and seven lakes available, anglers are assured of uncrowded conditions throughout the year. For further information contact: 7-Lakes Ranch, 738 County Road 59, Meeker, Colorado 81641. Phone: (303) 878-4722.

The Pices, Alaska

From where I sat I could hear nothing but the lapping of waves and the chirping of bald eagles. At least twenty of the regal birds perched in the nearby trees, strutted on the sandy beach and soared high overhead. A half dozen harbor seals cavorted in the water around me, and schools of silvery sockeye and pink salmon swam toward the mouth of little Anan Creek a few yards away.

I sat on the fantail of the Pices, sipped my after dinner coffee, and watched the sun sink slowly behind the mountains turning the sky, the clouds and the water pink, then red, and then purple. It was a time that could only be described with a cliché — "the perfect end of a perfect Alaskan day."

To most fly fishers, an Alaskan trip means a fly-out lodge, a week long river float, or a spike camp in the wilderness, and these are all, perhaps, the best way to see and fish Alaska for the first time or two. But for those seeking a new way to sample the wonders of this magnificent state, it would be hard to beat a cruise on the Pices.

The *M. V. Pices*, a very plush sixty-five foot north sea trawler — a yacht if you prefer, was formerly owned by the Smothers brothers. It is now owned and operated by Captain Bob Bergere and his wife Marilyn of Seattle, Washington. Though the Pices is their family boat, it is available for a limited number of charter fishing cruises each season and it provides a unique way to explore Alaska's remote and often un-fished streams.

My wife, Shirley, and I boarded an Alaska Airlines jet in Spokane, Washington and flew to Ketchikan to join Bob and Marilyn for a week of exploring aboard the Pices during mid-July. Our goal was to simply cruise northward along Alaska's inside passage, look for streams on the map, and go there to see what we would find. In all likelihood, we would fish water in which few, if any, had ever cast a fly. It was to be exploring in every sense of the word.

The Pices has a comfortable dining room and lounge complete with overstuffed chairs, a sofa, VCR television, stereo and all the comforts of home. Its compact galley is outfitted with a range, microwave, freezer, refrigerator, and all of the conveniences of any modern kitch-en. In short, it's a first class fishing lodge, but in this case, the lodge goes along with you. With its capacity of six guests plus the crew, the Pices is perfect for charter by a small group of friends or a couple of families.

Shirley and I quickly fell into the shipboard routine. We'd start the day with a leisurely breakfast as the Pices slipped her mooring and headed for a new destination. Then we'd take our coffee cups and cameras to the upper deck to enjoy the passing scenery as we eased into the day. We'd look for eagles, watch the porpoise that often bounded along side us, or scan the shoreline for bears or other wildlife. The cruising proved to be at least as enjoyable to us as the fishing.

If the spirit moved us, we would break out the saltwater gear that Bob provided and spend a little time trolling for salmon for our dinner.

When we reached the mouth of the stream we had targeted on the map, we'd get into our waders and assemble our fly rods, while Kim, Bob's daughter and our crew for the trip, lowered the Boston Whaler to take us ashore.

Since we were exploring, we never knew what awaited us. Sometimes we found a narrow stream rushing through the thick rain forest, and sometimes a broad river with long tidal pools. Sometimes the river was filled with little eight- to fourteen-inch rainbow trout that came readily to the dry fly, sometimes there were no fish at all, and sometimes the river would be black with sockeye or pink salmon, and we'd catch them until we tired of it. But in every case, the explora-tion was an adventure.

On one small creek we had the unusual pleasure of enjoying fishing and hiking along a stream that was covered with litter — the kind of lit-ter that I can tolerate. Wherever we looked, the ground was covered with eagle feathers, for the birds had been molting. We fished all day with huge eagle flight quills stuck in our hats, but took care to leave the feathers on the beach at the end of the day, for their possession is a federal offense.

It was on the same stream that we had another special adventure. We were fishing in a narrow pool below a small waterfall. The pool was filled with salmon, and I had just taken an eight pound sockeye and Shirley had landed a seven pound pink. I was involved with another salmon when I head Shirley say rather tentatively, "Dave." Then louder, "*Dave!*"

I looked up to see a huge bear stroll out of the woods and down to the stream across from us a mere thirty feet or so away. The bear glanced at us with only passing interest, lumbered into the stream, and snatched a salmon in its jaws. We stood transfixed, but for some reason, not at all frightened. The bear ambled back onto the stream bank, lay down and devoured the fish. Then it rose, stretched, and walked off up the river. Amazing!

The finish of that particular day was appropriately spectacular. We returned to the Pices just as Marilyn and Kim were pulling in the crab traps that we had set after breakfast, and they were filled with Dungeness crab. Kim soon had a tub of sea water boiling on the afterdeck, and she set about preparing a feast.

All of the meals aboard the Pices were special. We'd eaten steaks and salmon, and fresh halibut that we'd caught bottom fishing at our mooring. We'd had sourdough breads and hot cakes, and sweet corn and pies. In fact, the whole trip was a gourmet's delight. But the fresh crab topped them all. For the first time in my life I ate crab until I could hold no more, and there was still more to be eaten.

And so I found myself sitting on the fantail, sipping coffee, and enjoying the eagles, the harbor seals and the sunset. I had seen Alaska many times before, but never as I had seen it from the Pices.

The Pices' charter schedule begins with fly fishing for steelhead in April. May and June feature saltwater fishing for king salmon, and July is the month for freshwater fly fishing for sockeye and pink salmon. The season ends in August with saltwater fishing for silver salmon.

Rates, reservations and other information on chartering the Pices can be obtained from: Capt. Bob Bergere, 14004 Riviera Place, E. Seattle, Washington 98125 (206) 365-6438; or, Alaska Sportfishing Lodge Association, 500 Wall Street, Suite 401, Seattle, Washington 98121 (800) 352-2003.

Middle Fork of the Salmon River, Idaho

When the time for their annual family vacation rolls around, many families, especially those made up of both anglers and non-anglers, are faced with a dilemma. How can both factions be satisfied? What kind of vacation can be taken that would provide interest and excitement for those who like to fish as well as for those who do not?

Typically such a situation leads to many heated debates before finally being settled by a compromise in which no one is really happy.

It doesn't have to be that way, though. There is a solution to the problem which just might satisfy the entire family. In addition to the opportunities provided by the K Bar L and the 7-Lakes ranches, a float trip down the Middle Fork of the Salmon River is ideal.

The Middle Fork, designated as part of the Recreational Wild and Scenic River System in 1968, is born in a quiet alpine meadow high in the mountains of central Idaho. After slowly winding its way through the lush high country, it bursts over Daggar Falls and plunges into one of the deepest gorges in North America where it rushes and tumbles for over a hundred miles through the heart of the million and a half acre Idaho Primitive Area to join the main Salmon River. Dropping at an average of twenty-two feet per mile, the Middle Fork offers one of America's most exciting white water float trips.

Thrilling white water is not the river's only attraction, for its cold, clear depths are home to a pure strain of cutthroat trout that provide excellent sport for fly fishermen. The unique blend of floating and fishing through one of the country's most magnificent wilderness canyons provides a vacation opportunity that is almost certain to please any family.

The river can be reached by either of two methods. Many private parties drive to the Daggar Falls launch site over State Highway 21 from Stanley, Idaho, a distance of about forty miles. A shuttle is arranged to transport vehicles down to the confluence of the Middle Fork and main Salmon Rivers where the trip will end. In time of low water or for shorter trips, a charter flight can be arranged at the Boise Air Terminal that will fly parties to the Indian Creek landing strip adjacent to the river.

Though many private parties make the five to six day float each year, the trip is not for the poorly equipped or those inexperienced at white water rafting. Unless you have considerable experience at such things, a better approach is to float with a licensed guide and outfitter who will supply all of your food and equipment and will arrange the transportation. Such a trip is ideal for families, and provides an excellent opportunity for a real wilderness adventure for the inexperienced.

To preserve the quality of the wilderness experience as well as the environment, the number of parties allowed to begin a trip each day is strictly regulated, and each group is required to reserve a specific campsite for each night of the trip. Thus, while there may be many people on the river at a given time, they will be spaced sufficiently far apart so they will rarely see one another, and each group will be alone at the evening campsite. Reservations can be made through the Forest Service office listed at the end of the article. Of course, if you plan to float with a guided party, the reservations will be handled by the outfitter.

While the Middle Fork is not noted for its large fish, the fly fisherman can expect steady action from its population of fat streamed cutthroat trout which will run to over sixteen inches in length. An occasional Dolly Varden trout may be even larger. The fish are generally

The Middle Fork of the Salmon River, Idaho.

not selective feeders, and can usually be taken on a high riding size 10-14 dry fly such as a Goofus Bug, Royal Wulff, Caddis, or your favorite hopper pattern.

If the dries are not producing, a buggy looking nymph such as the Gold Ribbed Hare's Ear, Casual Dress, or Muskrat in sizes 8 to 14 will usually produce on a sinking tip line. A floating line can be used if the flies are weighted. Small marabou or matuka streamers or Muddler minnows are also effective.

Heavy snow run-off makes the river too dangerous to float in June, and early to late-July is best reserved for those primarily interested in the thrills of spectacular white water rafting. By the end of July, though, the water level drops and conditions improve for anglers through September.

My first experience on the Middle Fork came during early August several years ago, and it's hard to imagine that the timing could have been better. The hot days brought the grasshoppers to a peak of activity, and a probing artificial was sure to bring a strike when dropped into the patch of slick water behind every protruding boulder that we passed. The question was not so much would we get a fish, but how large would it be? Naturally, the fishing is not always that fast, but I have never been disappointed on the Middle Fork.

Special fishing regulations have been enacted to protect the pure strain of West Slope Cutthroat trout which inhabit the Middle Fork and its tributaries, and the entire river is open to artificial fly or lure, barbless hook, catch-and-release fishing only. As in other areas of the country, these regulations have been successful in helping the fish population to restore itself, and the fishing is now better than ever.

But a float down the Middle Fork is so much more than simply a fishing trip. It is a total wilderness experience the likes of which can rarely be found today. The river twists and churns its way between thousand foot high cliffs of sheer rock, and man and raft seem to shrink to insignifance before the awesome wonders of nature.

Eagles and ospreys soar overhead, mink and weasels scamper among the rocks, and big horn sheep stand and stare as you drift silently past. You can refresh yourself at Sunflower Flat where a thermal hot spring gushes over a cliff and cascades down to provide a natural hot shower, and you can climb to Indian caves and inspect eight-thousand-year-old petroglyphs painted across their walls.

You will shout for the pure joy of it as your big raft lifts, dives, and splashes through a succession of foaming rapids with such intimidating names as "Tappan Falls," "Artillery," "Cannon," and "Powerhouse," and you're almost certain to wish that you'd brought more film as you try to photograph the breathtaking beauty of this rugged country.

Though both the country and the river are wild, large, stable rafts and skilled boatmen insure that a float down the Middle Fork of the Salmon River is safe for almost anyone. However, families with children under the age of ten, or those with special medical problems should consult with the outfitter before booking a trip.

The Middle Fork of the Salmon may not be a Mecca for fly fishermen — there are many places in the West that will provide better fishing for bigger fish. But when it comes to combining top notch fishing and a white water float trip with the magnificent grandeur of a spectacular wilderness canyon, the Middle Fork of the Salmon River can't be beat. And best of all, it's an adventure the entire family can enjoy.

OUTFITTERS:

Idaho Outfitter and Guide Association, Inc.
P. O. Box 95
Boise, Idaho 83701

LANDING STRIPS AND FLIGHT INFORMATION:

Idaho Department of Aeronautics
2103 Airport Way
Boise, Idaho 83706

HUNTING AND FISHING REGULATIONS:

Idaho Fish and Game Department
600 S. Walnut Street
Boise, Idaho 83706

MAPS, RESERVATIONS AND TRIP INFORMATION:

Challis National Forest*
Forest Service Building
Challis, Idaho 83226
*This is the office that makes trip reservations.

Payette National Forest
Forest Service Building
P. O. Box 1026
McCall, Idaho 83638

Salmon National Forest
Forest Service Building
P. O. Box 729
Salmon, Idaho 83467

Columbia Basin Lakes, Washington

Feeling ridiculous is nothing new to me. I once attended a dressy Oriental dinner party where the guests were required to remove their shoes — and I was wearing white sweat socks beneath my dark suit and dress boots. Then there was the time I discovered my fly was open while I delivered a lecture to a class of a hundred amused young men and women. And once, while deeply engrossed in a conversation with a group of students, I pulled my lighter from my pocket, lit it, and put it to my face only to discover that I wasn't smoking my pipe.

But I'm sure that I've never felt more ridiculous than I did the first time I fished one of Washington State's Columbia Basin lakes. After all, a man winding his way through acre upon acre of desert sagebrush wearing chest waders, a fishing vest, and a landing net and carrying a fly rod in his hand and a float tube over his shoulder, would appear to be an almost certifiable mental case—especially when the temperature is almost ninety degrees and no water is visible as far as the eye can see. If he were asked where he was going and he replied, "trout fishing," he would almost certainly be placed in a home with padded walls and white-coated attendants.

As ludicrous as it appears, however, such a scene is routine for anglers who have discovered the Basin lakes of southeastern Washington.

The paradox of fly fishermen tromping through the desert was caused by the building of O'Sullivan Dam as a part of the Columbia Basin Project in the early 1950s. The tremendous pressure created as the huge Potholes Reservoir began to fill behind the new dam forced water deep into the porous volcanic strata of this arid land. Gradually, underground rivers began to flow, the water table shifted, and water trickled back to the surface in low spots many miles from the reservoir. Thus were born the desert "seep lakes."

The new lakes proved to be rich, and aquatic insect life took hold quickly. When the state game department began its stocking program in the mid- to late-sixties, fish growth rates were exceptional. There were tales of five- to seven-pound rainbows. Anglers flocked to the new lakes to share in the wealth.

As is typical of new impoundments, though, fish growth rates soon stabilized. Fishing pressure took its toll, and the average fish size decreased. By the mid-seventies fish averaged about fourteen inches in lakes where they had averaged several inches larger a few years earlier. To preserve the fishery, more stringent angling regulations were established in certain quality waters, and the decline in fish size has been reversed. Once again average fish size is increasing and in some lakes is close to sixteen inches.

The Lenice, Merry, and Nunnally Lakes chain near the villages of Royal City and Beverly, Washington—among the most popular with fly fishermen—is typical of the more than seventy seep lakes of the Columbia Basin that are managed for trout.

The lakes are not visible from the road, but anglers should have little difficulty locating their parking areas, which can be found on the Smyrna Road just east of Royal City, Washington. The road swings westward after leaving Royal City and in several miles changes from asphalt to gravel. A few miles farther on, a parking area sign on the north roadside announces Lake Lenice. The road continues west past parking areas for Merry and Nunnally Lakes before reaching the village of Beverly.

My early experiences on Lake Lenice occurred on a spring day several years ago on return from a business trip to western Washington. Somehow my float tube and fishing tackle had found their way into the car, and when I pulled into the parking area just after noon, I exchanged a three-piece suit for fishing togs and strode off across the desert on the quarter-mile hike to the lake.

Desert seep lakes, Washington.

As I crested a rise in the sandy trail, the lake spread out before me like a deep blue oasis. I had it all to myself.

Since no fish were rising, I rigged a sinking-tip line, tied on a black marabou leech and paddled out onto the lake. I was unfamiliar with the water, so I let the rising breeze carry me past a high rock outcrop and cast and drifted the fly as I moved slowly down the lake.

My enthusiasm waned considerably, however, after several hours of casting and changing fly patterns produced no results. The breeze had freshened into a wind, and as I was contemplating paddling my tube back across the long lake against the breaking waves, I discovered a small backwater among the weedbeds. The water, by some fluke, was glassy smooth, and a small dimple in its surface caught my eye as I pushed slowly through the tules.

I dismissed the disturbance as caused by a small fish, but it was quickly followed by a second rise some distance away. Before I could decide just what it was, I saw a dorsal fin, and the hair on the back of my neck rose. There was no mistaking the size of that fin.

It was not difficult to discover the cause of the activity, for when I leaned over in my tube and inspected the water, I could see its surface was covered by drifting midge pupae. I replaced my sinking-tip line with a floater carrying a long 5X leader, and a size 18 gray midge pupa. My first cast dropped lightly near where I'd seen the fish.

I started to draw the line back with an almost imperceptible retrieve when with a slurp a large fish rolled at the fly. My rod tip lifted automatically, met a solid resistance, and took a deep bend as a thick-bodied rainbow twisted into the air. I found myself looking *up* from my tube at the soaring trout. The ensuing fight has been described in angling literature countless times.

Time ceases when a large fish is being played under difficult conditions, and I have no idea how long we fought. Eventually, the broad trout slid over the edge of my landing net, and I sat quietly in my tube and admired its beauty for a moment before releasing it. It weighed something over four pounds.

It wasn't long before fish started rising again to the emerging pupae. Although the wind continued to whip across the main lake, my little cove remained calm, and I spent several rewarding hours working over gently sipping trout until the hatch ended.

I was lucky. Wind is an ever present problem on all of the desert lakes, and it can often cut short or entirely prevent fishing. More than once I have driven several hours from my home in Idaho only to sit in my car waiting for a wind that never dropped enough to fish. Occasionally the desert sand is churned into an all-out dust storm that makes even driving hazardous.

It's important to carry both light- and medium-weight tackle when fishing the seep lakes. When there is little wind, a rod balanced for 5- and 6-weight lines is ideal, but when the breeze starts to kick up, a 7- or 8-weight outfit is better.

The lakes are not deep, but a variety of sinking lines, as well as a floater, gives the flexibility needed to keep the fly at the right depth according to conditions. When the fish are taking on or near the surface, I prefer fairly long leaders (nine to twelve feet), with tippets to match the flies and conditions. On the other hand, when using sinking lines, I usually shorten the leader to as little as three feet. Often my entire leader will consist only of a butt section and an appropriate tippet. Such a configuration keeps the fly down to the depth of the line. I modify the leader-tippet arrangement as conditions require.

The desert lakes are fertile, containing a smorgasbord of trout foods. *Chironomidae*, mayflies, damselflies, dragonflies, leeches, freshwater shrimp and scuds can all be on the menu. The well-prepared angler is stocked with matching patterns.

In addition to the usual midge pupal patterns, a local favorite is the T.D.C. Nymph, created by Richard Thompson, a fisheries biologist with the U.S. Fish and Wildlife Service (see pattern recipes). The fly is deadly when fished in the surface film with an ultra-slow retrieve during a midge hatch.

When no fish are showing on the surface, I usually explore the water with either my pet black leech pattern or Grant's Green Weenie (see pattern recipes). The Weenie is a variation of the Carey Special, created in the early seventies by Grant Hendrickson. It is a stillwater favorite among Grant's friends who are familiar with it.

During a damselfly hatch nothing serves better than a Marabou Swimming Damsel (see pattern recipes). Allow the fly to sink close to the tops of the weedbeds, and then retrieve it with a series of short, rapid strips to produce a vigorous swimming motion. The fish hit it with a vengeance.

Some of the desert lakes can be reached by road, but many require a hike of from one-quarter to three-quarters of a mile. While some can be fished reasonably well from shore, flotation allows you to cover more water and increases your opportunity to locate fish. A canoe with a carrying yoke or a small pram with a pair of wheels mounted on the transom work well, but the ideal craft is the float tube.

The creator of the first float tube must have been a seep-lake fisherman. The portability of a float tube permits carrying all equipment to the lake in a single trip, and a tube provides excellent mobility on the water. There are no anchors or oars to contend with, you can fish constantly, and you can always be in just the right position.

No boat or floating devices equipped with motors are permitted on any of the lakes designated as Quality Waters by the state of Washington. Angling in Quality Waters is restricted to single, barbless-hook flies or lures and the bag limit is one fish per day. Due to the many lakes in this region, the variation in the seasons, limits, tackle and motor requirements, anglers should check regulation booklets before fishing unfamiliar waters.

In the past, many of the desert lakes were regulated under a split season. Opening occurred in late April and closure came in early July, with reopening on October 1 and running to the end of November. Since the 1982 season, however, the Quality Lakes have featured a single season between April 18 and November 30. The reduced harvest under stringent bag limits permits the longer season.

Summers are extremely hot in the desert and surface-water temperatures in the lakes become very high. The temperatures and excessive weed growth slow fishing during the hot months of July and August. But the single season allows fishing whenever the conditions are right and should eliminate the split-season Opening Day madness.

Although technically not a seep lake, Dry Falls Lake in the Sun Lakes area near Coulee City, Washington, deserves special mention. Prior to the ice age, the giant Columbia River thundered over a huge falls here on its way to the Pacific Ocean. Over four hundred feet high and 3½ miles wide, the falls would dwarf Niagara. With the coming of the ice age, the river was blocked upstream from the falls and its course shifted, leaving in its place the dry river bed and the skeletal remains of the awesome waterfalls.

Today the area is starkly beautiful. Magnificent basalt cliffs towering over the sand and sage of the valley floor are reflected in the still waters of Dry Falls Lake nestled at their feet. Where tons of water once crashed with a frightening roar, rainbow and brown trout now swim, and an angler floating in a tube is enveloped in silence.

The lake is accessible by a short, rough, gravel road running from the Sun Lakes State Park to the water's edge. Fly fishermen should be successful with the same tackle, flies and techniques described for the other lakes.

Convenient, though crowded, camping is available at Sun Lakes State Park. Shops and concessions are also available, and there is even a golf course for non-fishermen.

Accommodations while fishing the other desert lakes are not convenient. Anglers can either camp at unimproved sites near the parking area for each lake (bring your own water and firewood) or can stay at a motel in the nearest town, in some cases as much as thirty miles from the fishing.

Trout are not the only quarry to be found in the desert lakes. Some are managed for bass and other warm water species, and are open year-round. A number of lakes contain giant bluegill that average a half-pound and can run to over a pound. These lakes provide excellent angling for trout fishermen during the off season, but some folks pursue warm water species almost exclusively. Bassbugs and panfish poppers, as well as subsurface flies such as leeches, damsel nymphs and Woolly Worms produce when cast toward weedbed edges.

As with fishing anywhere, angling in the seep lakes of Washington can be a hit-or-miss proposition. A given lake might be red hot for a day or a week and then turn off the next. You might drive a hundred miles only to find the day so windy that you can't fish, or you might find no wind at all. A lake might be dead all day, but suddenly come to life in the last hour before dark. Or the fish might hit right at midday. As the man said, "The best time to go fishing is when you can get away," and that's certainly true of the seep lakes. And no matter how ridiculous you feel strolling across the desert in full fishing gear, you'll almost always find a rainbow at the end of the trail.

For additional information on the lakes of the Columbia Basin contact: Department of Game, Box 1237, Ephrata, WA 98823, (509) 754-4624.

SEEP LAKE FLY PATTERNS

Grant's Green Weenie

HOOK: size 2-12, weighted.

BODY: Olive blend of dyed rabbit and seal substitute.

HACKLE: Green rump feathers from a Chinese ring-neck pheasant tied moderately long.

Marabou Swimming Damsel (also see Chapter 20)

HOOK: size 8-10 short shank, wide gap (a bait hook is excellent). Cover hook shank with a double layer of fine lead wire.

BODY: Extended body of *sparse* olive marabou fibers.

THORAX: Peacock herl over length of hook shank.

WING CASE: (Optional) Dyed green mallard flank tied down over entire thorax.

LEGS: (Optional) Green mallard flank fibers tied moustache style ahead of thorax.

T.D.C. Nymph

HOOK: size 6-12, 1X-3X long.

BODY: Black chenille or wool tapered forward from about middle of hook bend.

RIB: Medium silver tinsel.

THORAX: Black chenille or wool built up to 1½ times the body thickness behind the thorax.

COLLAR: Three to four turns of white or cream ostrich herl ahead of thorax.

Marabou Leech (also see Chapter 20)

HOOK: size 4-8, weighted with double layer of lead fuse wire.

BODY: Extended body of longest black marabou tied in at bend of hook (long, soft and sparse). Hook shank covered with black angora or other fuzzy yarn (cement hook shank prior to wrapping yarn for durability).

11.

The Kid and the Kings

J eff stood silhouetted in the window of the air terminal, and I wondered what he was thinking as he stared intently out at the big Alaska Airlines jet that was about to take us on our next adventure.

I know what I was thinking. I was thinking of a wet, pink little creature letting out a howl with his first breath of life as I stood in awe in the delivery room. And I was thinking of a skinny little seven-year-old kid who had just caught his first trout on a fly — a magnificent six incher, and he was holding it up proudly for his dad to admire.

I was thinking of a trip into the Quetico–Superior country, and a smiling kid of eight in a canoe holding up a stringer full of smallmouth bass. I thought of a father and his twelve-year-old son skinny-dipping in an icy Montana creek, then lying naked on a warm rock to dry in the sun and to talk of the things fishing partners talk about.

I thought of a husky lad of fifteen winning a Federation of Fly Fishers fly casting contest with three casts that averaged 129 feet.

I thought of a tall young man in a red gown with a gold honors braid striding across a platform to receive his high school diploma just a few weeks earlier.

And I thought of what it was like to lose your best fishing partner. Oh, we'd still be buddies, and we'd have other adventures, but things would never again be quite the same. College, a job and a family of his own would be the new order of things. For the first time I realized how my father must have felt so many years ago.

For years Jeff and I had joked about "our trip to Alaska." We both knew that it would likely never happen, but it was fun to talk about by a campfire, or while we were walking along a little trout stream somewhere. "Boy, when we get to Alaska...," one of us would say. And the other one would grin, and wish that it could be so.

Now it was about to happen. As a high school graduation present for Jeff I had managed to arrange our dream trip. And so he stood looking out of that window thinking his thoughts, while I stared at him and thought mine.

"Passengers on Alaska flight 85 for Anchorage may now board. Please have your boarding passes ready."

Our destination was the Golden Horn Lodge in the Wood River-Tikchik Lakes region of Alaska, and after a brief stop in Anchorage, our plane continued on to the village of Dillingham where we were met by Bud Hodson who, along with his wife, Holly, was the manager of the lodge at that time. After loading our gear into Bud's float equipped Beaver, we took off for Jeff's first low level look at the magnificent wilderness that is Alaska.

Rivers and lakes, and mountains and tundra unfolded before us, and our eyes searched the ground below for moose, bear and other wildlife. And whether it is your first visit to Alaska or your tenth, the sights never fail to thrill you.

The Golden Horn, a large log lodge situated on Mikchalk Lake, has a capacity of eighteen to twenty guests, and is typical of Alaska's fine fly-out lodges. Its only access is by air, and most fishing is reached by float plane. The planes enable anglers to fish an area roughly the size of the state of West Virginia, provide a wide variety of fishing possibilities, and are almost a guarantee of fishing success.

Five species of salmon, plus rainbow trout, Arctic charr, Dolly Varden, Arctic grayling, northern pike and lake trout await the visiting angler, and combine to make Alaska truly the greatest fly fishing area on earth. The fishing is spectacular any time of the season, and the choice of when to make your trip should be determined by which type of salmon you wish to catch.

The king salmon are generally in the rivers from mid-June through July. Sockeye (reds) will be found from late June through July, chums (dogs) from July through early August, pinks (humpies) from mid-July through August, and silver salmon (coho) from August through September. Late August through September is also the time for trophy size rainbows.

Since Jeff and I were seeking the largest of the salmon, the big chinooks or kings, we had selected the first week of July for our adventure. The kings, which average twenty to twenty-five pounds and run to well over fifty pounds, are normally taken by anglers equipped with spinning or casting tackle, and they would provide the ultimate Alaskan challenge for our fly rods.

On the evening of our arrival, Jeff and I spread our tackle out on the lodge floor to organize it for our assault on the kings the next morning. We had brought heavy fly rods balanced for 10 weight lines, model 1495 Pflueger Medalist reels, a Pflueger Supreme salt water reel, fast sinking 10 weight (280 grain) shooting heads, and a variety of bright streamer flies tied on 3/0 and 5/0 salt water hooks. It was monstrous tackle, and looked as though it would handle anything that swam.

Our confidence in the tackle was short-lived, though. Several of the Golden Horn guides were watching our preparations, and they began to make casual comments regarding our lines and flies. "You know," one of them said, "we usually use a lot heavier shooting heads than those. This water is pretty heavy and to get down to where the fish are you'll need something like a 550-750 grain head."

"If you'd like a heavier reel, you could borrow one of my Fin-Nors."

"These are the flies we usually use for kings." The fly that he dropped into my hand weighed more than some of the trout that I catch, and it looked as though someone had wrapped a fluorescent orange chicken to the hook. It made my 5/0 models look positively dainty!

After a few minutes of such talk, it seemed apparent that the biggest tackle we owned might not be big enough for the kings, and Jeff said, "It sounds as though we're preparing for battle with no ammunition!" I had to agree.

Our first day in the pursuit of kings took us to the Nushagak River. The Nushagak is the major river for king salmon in the Brisol Bay region, and, according to Bud, it receives roughly 80 percent of the run. As the guides had indicated, it was big water. Though there were relatively few kings in the river on that day, the spin fishermen did fairly well, and took fish to about thirty-five pounds. We were not so fortunate.

After a hard day of casting both from the river bank and from a drifting boat, Jeff had managed to take only one small king and a seven pound sockeye. I had caught one chum of about ten pounds. It was obvious that our 280-grain high-density shooting heads were simply not getting deep enough. The heavy current would sweep the flies downstream before they had an opportunity to reach the depth of the fish. But, though our morale had slipped a little, we knew that we still had an entire week ahead of us in which to try to solve the problem.

We didn't try for kings again for a couple of days. On the second day, the normal rotation of guests took us to the Agulapak River, a beautiful piece of water, where Jeff took his first grayling and charr, and we caught rainbows to 4½ pounds. A side trip to the mouth of Moose Creek also gave us excellent fishing for northern pike to ten pounds — Jeff's first pike on a fly.

Our third day found us alone on one of my favorite little Alaskan streams. Except for the tundra, it could as well have been a small Montana spring creek, and it was loaded with two to six pound rainbows. Using floating lines with greased muddlers, we took turns fishing through its long pools and riffles, shouting back and forth in pure joy. And we slowed our pace only a little when we came upon a very large and very fresh grizzly track. It was the stuff of which Alaskan dreams are made.

But the big kings were never far from our minds, for they were what we had come to Alaska to catch, and the fourth day found us back on the Nushagak. This time, though, we had come better prepared. We had borrowed 750-grain high-density shooting heads from one of the guides, and had tied up a batch of new flies that were heavily weighted and more fully dressed.

The previous day one of the lodge guests had expressed an interest in learning to fly fish, and Bud had given him a quick casting lesson.

Then, with a borrowed rod and a broken reel, he had made his first fly cast ever while fishing and proceeded to catch a thirty-two pound king! Needless to say, his experience had us convinced that this would be the day to tie into the kings.

But it was not to be. Though we drifted many miles of the river in a boat, made hundreds of casts from the bank, and fished until we were exhausted, our total catch for the day was Jeff's lone ten pound chum salmon. Again, the spin fishermen did fairly well, but there seemed to be relatively few kings in the river. The fishing was definitely slower than would normally have been expected for this time of the year.

On the fifth day Bud suggested that a change in tactics was in order if we were ever to be successful with the kings under the conditions that existed. With Bud as our guide, we headed for new water.

After setting the Beaver down in a small pond, we followed Bud across the tundra until he suddenly dropped to his knees, and then crawled on his belly up to the edge of a high clay bank. The Rawlings River, a modest little stream, curved through the brush below us, and as Bud pointed to the water, we could see that it was filled with dark pods of kings finning slowly in the current. We could sense that our luck was about to change.

We scarcely noticed the light drizzle that had begun to fall as we peered over the edge of the clay bank, watched the great fish, and planned our strategy. Bud would stay up on the bank to direct our casts, while Jeff and I would hike upstream, cross well above the pool, and then get into casting position. We rigged eight weight rods with sinking-tip lines, secured lightly weighted orange streamers to our tippets, and prepared to do battle.

When we were finally in position, Jeff stepped carefully into the pool, while I stayed behind with the camera to record the event for posterity. At Bud's direction, Jeff worked his line out, dropped the fly to the water at the head of the pool, and his body tensed as the fly drifted through the school of kings. Nothing.

Three more casts duplicated the first, before Bud yelled, "He looked at it! Give it to him again!"

Another cast.

"He's moving toward it — strike!!!"

The water erupted and all three of us shouted in unison — "All right!!!"

The shallow stream offered no depth for the fish, and it took to the air in a twisting leap before giving music to the reel with a powerful run. The tide of the fight turned many times until the big fish seemed to tire. Jeff put all of the pressure on the fish that the rod would stand, and just as he was about to land it, the king once again leaped into the air, and a loud *crack* sounded as the rod broke at the ferrule.

The salmon headed downstream with a rush, Jeff grabbed the line in his hands, and continued the battle without a rod. At last the spent salmon lay gasping on its side. Scooping it up in his arms, Jeff clasped

Author's son, Jeff, with thirty pound plus, Alaskan king salmon. "The Kid and the King."

the prize to his chest. It weighed twenty pounds.

The remainder of the day was a fitting climax to our adventure of a lifetime. We walked slowly along the narrow stream stalking the big kings, casting to individual fish or fishing blindly to likely looking water. We landed salmon of from fifteen to twenty-five pounds and broke off some that were much larger. Then, as the day neared its end, a huge boil engulfed Jeff's drifting fly.

Jeff, by that time an experienced king fisherman, parried the fish's every thrust with skillful moves of his own, while Bud and I shouted encouragement and often conflicting advice. Jeff brought the great fish to hand despite our help, tailed it, and lifted it from the water. The salmon topped thirty pounds and was the largest fish Jeff had ever taken.

It was a mighty proud young man who stood to have his picture taken with that salmon, and an even prouder father who watched him put it gently back into the water and nurse it back to life before releasing it to continue on its spawning run.

During our week at the Golden Horn, Jeff and I learned a great deal about fly fishing for Alaskan king salmon, both from our own experiences and from picking the brains of Bud and the guides.

We found that, when fishing the big water of the Nushagak and similar rivers, the most critical factor was to get the flies down quickly to the depth of the fish. Fly patterns were not critical—any big weighted streamer of red or orange feathers, hair or marabou would do the trick, but it had to be deep. Thus, anglers should be prepared with a range of shooting heads in various weights from 280 to 750 grains.

Such lines will require rods capable of casting at least a 10 weight line (280 grain). With the heavier heads, the casting is not artful — more of a "sling," actually, but what is lost in style and grace is made up for with increased effectiveness.

While high quality saltwater reels such as the Fin-Nor are certainly pleasant to use, and would probably be helpful with the really big kings, they are not required for the average fish — don't buy such a reel if you have no other need for it. Any well made reel with a large line capacity such as the Medalist model 1495 or 1495½ will do the job nicely. Plan on mounting your line ahead of at least 150 yards of stout backing.

In the smaller rivers such as the Rawlings, eight weight rods carrying high density sinking-tip lines will generally fill the bill.

Handling the flies in big water is primarily a matter of casting up and across the river, letting the fly sink, and stripping on the retrieve and swing. Bud often likes to walk the fly downstream as it is sinking to gain more depth, and then he stops to let it swing. The kings will often hit just as the fly begins to swing, but they'll also take it on the stripped retrieve.

Fishing the smaller rivers calls for a more sophisticated technique. The "dead drift" is often the most effective method, but, as Bud says, "you have to keep right on top of your fly." That is, the line must be kept almost tight and straight between the rod tip and the fly, and the line should be mended often to allow the fly to drift through the "slot" to the fish — an often difficult maneuver with large, heavy streamers.

Though the kings will sometimes hit a fly quite vigorously while it is being retrieved when you're fishing big water, the take is more often very gentle, and such is almost always the case when fishing the smaller streams. Thus, it is very important to watch the portion of your line that you can see for any abnormal pause, movement, change of direction, or slack — the same technique used when fishing a nymph dead drift for trout. If you feel the take, you may well be too late with your strike.

We found that when Bud was observing the drift of our flies from a good vantage point, he would often indicate that a fish had taken the fly when we were totally unaware of it. And by the time he'd yell at us and we'd strike, we had missed another fish. The tackle is large and the flies heavy and bulky, but the technique is very subtle.

Fishing for "bright" kings is primarily a phenomenon of the Bristol Bay region of Alaska, and the "bright" fish are found mainly at the lower ends of the rivers near the saltwater. Once the fish have been in fresh water for any length of time and have moved well into the drainage, they turn dark red. Though the catching and eating quality of the kings is still quite good until they are fairly close to spawning time, the strength and beauty of the "bright" fish make them the more desirable quarry.

In the Nushagak, fishing for kings begins to get good about June

15th and continues through the end of July. The run on the Togiak starts a little later. Fly fishermen can expect to have the best opportunity to take fish during the last half of the run—say after July 1, since there will be more fish in the rivers, and anyone planning to travel to Alaska specifically to catch kings, would be well advised not to make the trip after mid-July.

Fly fishing for king salmon is an exciting and challenging endeavor, and the well prepared angler stands a much better chance of success than one who is unprepared. Big, bright flies, good tackle, a wide range of sinking heads, persistence and the ability to make long casts all help to insure success. Under the best of conditions, only a small number of fish will be hooked, and fewer still will be landed. But it's those few that are the things of which memories are made.

Yes, I lost my long time fishing partner after our king salmon safari to Alaska, but I think that we've got him launched into life in the real world in pretty good shape. He's a crack wing shot, plays a great game of pool and a mean guitar, and he's a heck of a fly fisherman. He'll do O.K.

And every time I look at the picture of the smiling young man holding the big fish that hangs above my desk, I'll think of the kid and the kings, and of our great times together.

12.

On the Loss of Virginity

Most anglers worthy of the name are fully capable of holding an audience spellbound as they describe in the most minute detail the incredible events surrounding the capture of their first trout on a fly. They can rhapsodize on the brightness of the day, the form and color of the adversary, and their innermost feelings at the moment of truth.

Unfortunately, on that score, I'm a failure. Try as I might, I simply cannot recall my first trout taken on a fly. By some horrible stroke of fate, the moment that changed my life is forever lost to me.

But, perhaps I'm not a total failure. It still may be possible to redeem myself with my brothers of the angle with the following tale.

The day I'll not forget found me driving down a steep winding road just as the sun burst into the magnificent canyon. The streaming yellow rays turned the landscape to a glittering gold as I dropped ever deeper between the steep hills, and I stabbed at the brakes when the first covey of chukar partridge that I'd ever seen wandered aimlessly across the road in front of me. I stopped and watched until they all disappeared into the thick cheatgrass along the roadside.

Upon reaching the river, I, too, wandered aimlessly upstream looking for just the right piece of water. I wouldn't have been able to explain just what I was looking for, but would know it when I saw it.

The sun was full upon the water when I finally stopped the car, inspected the rippling water, and decided that I had found the place.

My long rod was quickly assembled, and the heavy line threaded through the guides. The naked leader point hung limply in my hand as I inspected my fly book and finally selected the only fly of its type whose name I knew for certain.

The leader was bent to the fly with little ceremony, and soon I was thigh deep in the cold, clear water enjoying the familiar feeling of "oneness" with the environment. The slender rod worked in a steady rhythm of the false casts, until it suddenly stopped. The line shot forward, and a shower of spray danced in the sunlight.

How many times the gentle scene repeated itself I cannot say. It played itself over and over like a broken phonograph record and time seemed to be suspended. I stood thus for perhaps twenty or possibly thirty minutes before it happened, and when it finally did, it took me

in the usual manner — by surprise. The line suddenly went tight, the rod arched, and my wrist responded without the benefit of a command from my brain. I recognized the powerful surge of a big fish, and yet I knew this one was different.

The reel screamed as it always does in these stories, and the tempo of the placid scenario abruptly accelerated as the record skipped from its broken groove. Again, as is typical of these tales, the line seemed to melt from the reel spool as the fish bolted downstream before shattering the smooth surface of the water with an arching, twisting leap amidst a shower of spray. And I saw my fish.

Its broad side gleamed as freshly minted sterling in the bright sunlight, and a tingle raced down my spine.

The battle was typical, and yet unique. It was my first. The big hen fish ran. She jumped. She rolled on the surface. She ran again and again. And, finally, she turned on her side in utter exhaustion.

My hands shook when it was over, and I gently laid my fish on a nearby rock. Almost as an afterthought, I spread a few fresh daisies by her side, and took a portrait of the most beautiful fish I had ever seen.

The Skykomish Sunrise still hung from the corner of her mouth, and I stood beside Washington's Grande Ronde River gazing down at my first steelhead taken on a fly.

There have been other days and other fish since that first. As might be expected, I've learned a few things since then, and, of course, I'm still learning.

One thing I've discovered is that steelhead flies have a tradition and a mystique all their own. Their numbers are probably uncountable, many of their names are rather unpronounceable, and some of their materials almost unobtainable. Every fisherman has his own favorites, and they all seem to catch fish.

Like most steelheaders, I carry several books full of a wide variety of flies. After all, they are very pretty! But, frankly, most of them are just there to look at. Most of my fishing for summer run fish is done with only four or five different patterns, and, of course, I have my own theory on when each should be used.

Basically, my theory is this. In clear water on a bright day, I first try either my "super fly" or a bright pattern. If the day and the water are both dark, I try a dark fly first. In clear water on a dark day I start with my "super fly." Thus, I need at least three patterns, a bright fly, a dark fly, and my "super fly."

For a bright fly I really have no choice. That has to be the Skykomish Sunrise simply because that fly took my first steelhead as described above. A good second choice when a slightly more sparse fly is desired is the Tulley version of the Polar Shrimp. Both have a place in my book.

The dark fly that's number one in the waters I fish is unquestionably the Skunk. It gets the nod from me, too.

My "super fly?" I thought you'd never ask! The Purple Peril. In my "home waters" in Idaho this fly has accounted for more fish for my partners and me than any other single fly we use. I can't explain why...it just does, dang it! Maybe we have more faith in the fly, use it more often, or fish it more thoroughly. For whatever the reason, it's become my number one fly.

Then, if you peer way back in a dark corner of my book, you'll see the Nameless Wonder...a floating steelhead fly. That's right, a floater! If you haven't tried greased line fishing on top for summer run steelhead, you have not yet begun to live. Steelhead do come up to the top for a fly, and they come up hard! Dust off an old copy of Jock Scott, read it, and then go steelheading. You may never be the same!

The patterns for my "fearsome fivesome" are listed below. If you are already a steelheader, you no doubt have your own list of favorites. But, if you are just beginning your pursuit of this fantastic fish, you're welcome to my list. They'll stand you in good stead.

SKYKOMISH SUNRISE

Hook: Buz's Special 2X Stout - 1X Long, Nickel plated* Sizes, 2, 4, 6

Tail: Mixed scarlet and yellow hackle wisps

Body: Fluorescent red or orange chenille with flat or oval silver tinsel rib

Hackle: Mixed scarlet and yellow

Wing: Polar bear or white bucktail

*This hook is available from Buz's Fly and Tackle Shop, 805 W. Tulare Ave., Visalia, California 93277.

SKUNK
>   Hook: As above
>   Tail: Scarlet hackle wisps
>   Body: Black chenille with flat or oval silver tinsel rib
>   Hackle: Black
>   Wing: Polar bear or white bucktail

PURPLE PERIL
>   Hook: As above
>   Tail: Purple hackle wisps
>   Body: Purple floss or wool yarn with flat or oval silver tinsel rib
>   Hackle: Purple
>   Wing: Natural deer body hair tied fairly sparse

POLAR SHRIMP
>   Hook: As above
>   Tail: Red hackle wisps
>   Body: Rear half flat gold tinsel; front half orange chenille
>   Wing: Polar bear or white bucktail
>   Hackle: Orange saddle hackle dressed full, with one inch of the
>   hackle tip laid back over the wing as topping.

NAMELESS WONDER
>   Hook: sizes 2 to 6, 2X-4X Long
>   Tail: Deer or elk body hair
>   Body: Any color dubbing to suit your taste (or lack of it) try orange
>   for a starter.
>   Wing: Deer or elk body hair, tied spent
>   Hackle: None
>   Head: Deer or elk body hair clipped muddler style. (Grease well,
>   tie it on, and look out!)

NOTE: In tying the first three patterns, the hackle is generally wound on as a collar *before* the wing is tied in. In tying the Polar Shrimp, the hackle is tied in after the wing so the hackle tip can be dressed back as topping.

13.

Tackle and Tactics
For Low-Water Trout

Late-season fishing often presents the angler with low-water situations that require special tactics and considerable forethought, both before and after arriving at the area he or she has planned to fish. Low-water angling can be tough, but it is a situation the fly rodder can measure up to — and actually take advantage of.

During the late season, fish may tend to concentrate in small areas, making them more accessible to the fly fisherman. In addition, the cleaner water often provides opportunities for better fishing in some of the larger rivers where normal discoloration is usually a handicap. These same conditions, however, tend to make the fish extremely wary and super-selective. Thus, the paradox: fish are more available in the waters which remain, but they are more difficult to catch.

For the sophisticated fly fisherman, the situation provides an exciting challenge; unfortunately, those with less experience might face a great deal of difficulty and frustration unless care is taken to modify tackle, technique and strategy to meet these more demanding conditions.

A change from what may be your usual tackle, while not absolutely essential, can improve your ability to fish effectively under low-water conditions.

While the short midge rod still has many advocates and can be a joy to use under the appropriate circumstances, longer rods — 8 to 9½ feet or even longer — are enjoying a well-deserved resurgence of popularity, and are ideally suited to the problems confronting the low-water angler. Such rods help to avoid drag by permitting more line to be held off the water during the fly's drift. They permit longer casts with less effort, and they also allow you to keep your backcast high — important considerations at times of low water. At the same time, the rod, while longer, should be balanced for a light-weight line. A 2-, 3- or 4-weight line will simply produce less disturbance on the water than a 7- or 8-weight; the difference can be significant when casting to spooky trout.

The final link in the system, the leader, also requires modification. Most anglers are aware of the need for longer leaders when fishing for wary trout in clear water, and leaders of twelve to fourteen feet are commonly used under these conditions. A leader properly tapered for such lengths will turn over every bit as easily as one of 7½ to 9 feet. To accommodate the smaller flies generally used during low water, leaders should be tapered to at least 5X, and smaller when possible.

An excellent low water leader is the one designed by George Harvey, the well-known Pennsylvania angler, for use in his state's fabled limestone spring creeks. The "Harvey Leader," described in Chapter 27, departs radically from traditional freshwater designs in that it begins with a very light butt section. While such a taper requires a little more "punch" on the cast, it falls to the water in a beautiful series of serpentine curves, producing slack that can reduce drag on the fly. It is extremely effective under the most difficult conditions.

Though mayfly activity may be sharply reduced during the hot summer months, the trout continue to feed vigorously on those insects which are available — the terrestrials. And the angler who is astream with the proper tackle and a fly box well stocked with terrestrial imitations can experience some very fine fishing indeed.

Terrestrials, in contrast with aquatic insects, which spend a portion of their life cycles in the water, are land insects, which do not normally live in the water. They do find their way into the water, though. They are blown in, fall in, jump in, are knocked in, or they become fatigued while flying. They must taste good, too, or maybe it's because other food is scarce, but for whatever reason, trout take the stranded terrestrials with great relish.

It has been estimated that there are over eighty-two thousand species of terrestrial insects in North America. Major groups include the ants, beetles, caterpillars, crickets, grasshoppers, leafhoppers, and the various flying bees, wasps, deer flies, house flies, moths, and...well, you get the picture. The variety of terrestrial insects which find their way into trout streams is almost beyond the imagination.

Despite the large numbers of naturals that are available to the trout, the angler can do well with relatively few patterns. My own terrestrial box is stocked with various sizes of black and brown ants, black and brown beetles, grasshoppers, black crickets, bees, and a pattern to represent the black flying insects. A few green "inch worms" and some miscellaneous patterns complete the collection. With the exception of the 'hoppers, crickets, inch worms, and a few of the odd patterns, most of the artificials are tied on light wire hooks from size 14 through 22 with some even smaller.

The technique for fishing the terrestrials depends, of course, upon which pattern is being used. The angler must attempt to fish the artificial so it closely resembles the natural insect in action (or lack of action), line of drift, and position on or in the surface film of the water.

Grasshoppers, for example, can be found anywhere on the water, but they will often "splat" to the surface, and then lie still as if stunned for a few seconds. Then they kick furiously as they try to swim to the bank. They'll kick, rest, kick again, and then pause to rest. Thus, your artificial should be fished in the same manner, and placed so it will drift through good holding water for fish. Be ready for a vicious strike at any time, but especially just as you begin a twitch following a short pause.

Grasshoppers generally don't become active until the morning sun has warmed them a bit, so if you're fishing during the early hours, try a similar pattern in all black to represent a cricket, and fish it as you would the 'hopper.

In contrast to the 'hoppers and crickets, the ants and beetles generally drift quietly in the surface film, and are often found next to the bank near overhanging grass or brush. Patterns should be dressed to permit them to float flush with the surface film, but they should be greased well to prevent them from sinking. Cast a slack line and leader, and fish them dead drift along the edges of currents, scum patches, or the bank itself.

The rise to a quietly drifting ant or beetle will usually be merely a delicate sip which will produce only a small ring on the water even from a very large fish. Be alert for such a rise, or to any disappearance of the fly, and respond by simply lifting the rod to tighten the line. A hard, fast strike to set the hook will be unnecessary and may break off the fish. Look, too, for these subtle rise forms which will signal a feeding fish as you search the stream for activity. And remember, a large fish will rise very quietly when it's feeding on small terrestrials.

The proper tackle and flies are only part of the solution to the low-water angling problem. Next we must find the fish, and to do so we must consider three important variables: adequate cover, suitable water temperature and the oxygen content of the water. When these variables are considered for any given stream, a great deal of unproductive water can be bypassed and fishing time used most productively.

When the water level drops, fish may be forced to move from their normal habitat to seek new shelter. Look for them to be concentrated in deep pockets, scooped-out depressions next to rocks and in shallow water under logs and overhanging branches.

Low water will also warm considerably, and if the water temperature increases to above the tolerance level of the trout (approximately seventy-two to seventy-five degrees Fahrenheit), the fish must seek cooler water. In addition, as the water temperature rises, its ability to retain dissolved oxygen diminishes, forcing the fish to relocate to areas offering a higher oxygen content. Thus, a water thermometer becomes an important tool for the summertime angler.

A series of temperature readings along a stream will determine whether or not the water will support trout, and will help you find where cooler springs enter the stream. Find the cool water, and you're apt to find the fish. When the water temperature is near the upper limit for trout, try fishing the riffles and areas of white water which will be more adequately oxygenated. Well-shaded sections of the stream should also hold more fish than those sections exposed to the direct rays of the hot sun.

During most shallow-water periods, fish are reluctant to show themselves in the middle of the day, and early morning or late afternoon and evening fishing is generally the most productive. These hours also offer the coolest summer temperatures.

Late-summer fishing, like spring-creek fishing, is actually similar to hunting. The angler must literally become a "stalker." In low, clear water, trout seem to become nervous and tense, and will dart for cover at the slightest provocation. Extreme caution must be exercised when approaching a stream under these conditions. A major problem for the fisherman is to approach the fish without frightening it.

With this in mind, even the way we dress becomes important. Light-colored shirts, hats, and vests should be avoided in favor of darker colors which blend into the landscape. Belt buckles, pins, fly boxes, and ferrules can flash a long-distance warning to fish, and should either be eliminated or darkened with flat-black paint or nonreflective tape.

Let one word be your guide — *sneak*! Keep as low a profile as possible by bending over or crawling on your knees, and by moving slowly. Be aware of your background and keep trees or brush behind you whenever possible so you will not stand out against an empty skyline. If this is not possible, try to keep the bright sun at your back — trout don't like to look into it any more than you do, and it will help to cover your approach. But when doing this, you must not let your shadow fall across the fish or its lie; your shadow will spook it immediately.

Wherever possible, avoid wading; instead, attempt to find a suitable casting position along the bank. Even grinding gravel underfoot while wading will frighten fish, as will waves created on the surface. If you must wade, do so very carefully. Also, when wading, it is often difficult to avoid spooking unseen smaller trout which, in turn, frighten the one you were stalking. Stay on the bank if you can. (But walk softly, vibrations from your feet can also spook fish!)

You may find yourself faced with a variety of casting problems from the bank, however. You may be on your knees, sitting, or even lying down, and the longer rod I mentioned previously will be very helpful.

Having come this far, your low-water problems still aren't over. You have yet to present the fly to the fish, and that can be the toughest test of all! Under the most extreme conditions, even a false cast in the air over a fish can send it streaking for cover, so, as with every other aspect of the game, the watchword must be caution.

Make your false casts well to the side of the fish rather than directly in front of it, and, when making the presentation, drop the fly so that it drifts to the near side of the fish. If the hatch is sparse or nonexistent, he may move to the side to take the fly. If this fails, successive casts should be moved closer to his feeding lane. When this becomes necessary, use every trick at your disposal to avoid spooking the fish by putting your line directly over him. A good curve cast can be very helpful in this situation (See Chapter 26). Occasionally, a downstream presentation may be effective, but you may only have one opportunity to try it, because the pick-up may spook the fish if he fails to take your first effort.

Low-water fish will also be more critical of a dragging fly, so again, you must resort to your bag of tricks to avoid the problem. Reach casts, serpentines, puddle casts, "kick-backs" and upstream mends can all be used effectively to avoid drag, and each has its place in the complete angler's arsenal.

Summer and fall angling can be either a bust or a bonanza for the low-water angler, depending upon how well he or she adapts to a difficult situation. With the proper planning, a little casting practice, a fly box filled with terrestrials imitations and a thoughtful approach to the stream, it can be the very best time of the season.

14.

The Beetle:
My Ace-in-the-Hole Fly

T hink back to the times you've examined the contents of a trout's
stomach in an attempt to discover what it had been eating. What
did you find? If the fish had been feeding heavily, you quite likely
found a mass of insects — some specific species of mayfly, caddis, or
other item that was featured on the day's menu. But was there
anything else?

If you looked closely, you may have discovered, in addition to the
major dietary item, a beetle or two.

The discovery of an occasional beetle amid the mass of other insects
in a fish's stomach happened to me often enough to finally make me
realize that beetles must taste very good to trout. Rarely do trout have
the opportunity to eat beetles exclusively, but the bugs seem to be taken
readily when they're available, even when the fish are feeding primarily upon some other insect.

My introduction to beetles came many years ago while I was living
in central Pennsylvania's limestone country. At that time, the Jassid
was a popular pattern and it was a fair representation of the flat,
rounded shape of a beetle, and the fly produced very well for me. But
the Jassids weren't very durable, and, when it became all but impossible to obtain the jungle cock "nails" which the pattern required, I knew
that I had to develop a new fly that was both stronger and whose
materials were more readily available.

My first attempts merely used lacquered feathers from other birds
as a substitute for the jungle cock and were tied in the traditional
"jassid style." While this was reasonably effective, it still wasn't the effect I was seeking.

The real answer came one evening as I was tying the wing case of a
nymph and realized that with a little modification, the case would
look exactly like a beetle. That nymph was never finished. Instead, the
hook was replaced with a light wire size 18 dry fly hook, and my first
little beetle quickly took shape. I knew that I had found the answer to
my Jassid problem, and the pattern has remained virtually unchanged
to this day.

A very simple fly to tie, "my beetle" requires only a narrow section
from the secondary quill of a duck, goose, or turkey, and a dry fly

Beetle: Tie in flight quill section (dull side forward) and hackle at the bend of the hook).

Beetle: Palmer hackle over hook shank, and clip off short on top. Clip bottom to approximately half the gap of the hook.

Beetle: Fold the shell forward and tie off. Two fibers of the shell may be left as antennae.

The Beetle.

quality hackle feather of matching color. While black is my favorite color, both brown and mottled turkey also produce excellent beetles.

Begin with the tying thread at the rear of a size 16-18 dry fly hook and tie in a narrow section from the wing quill of a duck, goose, or turkey. The section should be tied in so it lies flat and extends back from the bend of the hook with the dull side facing up.

Wrap the hook shank with tying thread, and tie in a dry fly quality hackle feather about two-thirds of the hook length back from the eye of the hook. The dull side of the feather should face the tyer. Normally I prefer to use an oversize hackle for the beetle and then trim it to the proper length when the fly is completed, as I feel this gives the beetle stiffer legs and more support on the water. Coat the hook shank with head cement. Before the cement dries, palmer the hackle dry fly style over the middle one-third of the hook shank and tie it off. Clip off the excess hackle feather and trim the palmered fibers flat along the top of the hook. This should leave fibers projecting to both sides and the bottom of the fly.

Fold the quill section forward over the hook and tie it off near the eye. This will form the beetle's "shell." The shiny side of the quill section should now be on top of the fly. Without cutting off the excess quill that protrudes forward from the eye, whip finish the head, and cut off the tying thread. With a dubbing needle or the point of your scissors, separate one strand from each side of the quill section which is projecting forward from the hook. Clip out the center quill section leaving the two separated strands as antennae. Clip the antennae to length. (Actually, I've never seen antennae on a beetle, but they look so darn cute that I put them on anyway! Maybe they represent pinchers.)

To complete the fly, trim the hackle from its underside to about half the length of the gap of the hook, and if oversized hackle was used, trim the legs, i.e., the remaining hackle which projects from the side of the fly, to an appropriate length. The hackle should not be clipped too short on the belly of the fly to aid its floatability. Adequate hackle, plus a good coat of floatant such as Gink, LTP, or Mucilin will allow the fly to float very well.

While the beetle is quite simple to tie, a couple of special techniques are required to eliminate potential problems and to insure consistent results. First, it is important that the width of the quill section be appropriate for the size of the fly being tied. For a size 16 hook, the quill width should be 3/16 to 1/4 inch, and it should decrease as the fly size is reduced. Some experimentation will probably be required to find exactly the right width for the various hook sizes. I have found that it is very difficult to tie a fly larger than size 16 by this method, but it works very well down through size 28. If I require a beetle larger than size 16, I usually tie one of clipped or folded deer hair.

To produce a symmetrical shape to the beetle's shell, the technique used to tie in the quill section is also very important. The following process works quite well. Begin with the quill section held on its edge between the thumb and first finger of the left hand near the bend and on your side of the hook. The dull side of the feather should face you. Make a *loose* turn of the tying thread over the quill section and the hook, then *squeeze the quill, thread, and hook tightly* between your thumb and index finger as you draw the tying thread tight and roll the quill section onto the top of the hook shank. Bind the quill down with additional turns of thread, but *be certain that all turns after the initial one are taken forward from the first one*, i.e., toward the eye of the hook. If any turns of thread are allowed to go behind the original wrap, the quill section will fold or twist out of shape. If the shape is not symmetrical where the section is tied in, check to be sure you are squeezing it tightly as the thread is drawn tight.

The quill section should be tied in at the front of the hook in a similar manner. That is, make a loose turn of thread around the hook and the quill and then squeeze everything tightly between the left thumb and index finger while pulling the tying thread tight. The quill section will, of course, be lying in a horizontal plane during this step. Again, all future turns of the tying thread are taken in front of the original turn at the head.

In almost every case where problems are encountered with forming the beetle's shell, they will be either due to not squeezing the section tightly enough when tying it in, or to taking subsequent turns of thread behind the original wrap.

It is also important to palmer the hackle only over the middle third of the hook shank. If this is not done, the folded shell will deflect hackle fibers so they project forward and backward at odd angles and ruin the appearance of the legs.

Since I first realized just how much trout like to eat beetles, this pattern has become my ace-in-the-hole fly in many difficult angling situations in all parts of the country. If I'm fishing to rising trout in still water, and they show little interest in the fly which, to me, appears to be a good imitation of the natural—I tie on a beetle. If they aren't taking what I think they're taking, I don't have a close match for the natural, or I don't know what they're taking—I try a beetle. Or, as so often happens after a major hatch is over and the big "bank feeders" are sipping insects from the wind row of bugs that have collected along the edge of a stream—a beetle is usually my number one choice. And in the late summer when most of the hatches are over and terrestrials make up a large portion of a trout's diet, you guessed it! I opt for my box of beetles. You should, too.

15.

Fine and Fussy Fishin'

For as far as the eye can see, the glassy surface of the stream is broken by dozens of dimples and rings that mean only one thing to a fly fisherman...rising trout! Your eyes scan the air above the water, but see nothing. Not until you reach the edge of the stream do you observe the hundreds of tiny, mosquito-like flies dancing above the water.

You smile to yourself as you tie on a 6X tippet and produce a size 20 dry fly from your fly box. This is going to be like shooting ducks in a barrel.

Twenty, fifty, a hundred casts and half a dozen fly changes later and you're still waiting for your first "sitting duck." What can possibly be wrong? The fish are still rising. They haven't spooked, but they won't rise to your dry fly. What should you try next?

Look a little more closely, friend! Are the trout really taking dry flies from the surface, or could they be feeding on something else?

It takes a sharp eye to differentiate between a rise to a minute fly on the surface or to an insect just under the surface film. If all of the trout fishermen who have been fooled by this situation were laid end to end they'd probably line both banks of every stream in the country!

This is what the British refer to as a "smutting rise," and it commonly occurs when the trout are feeding on the pupal stage of the "midge." The "midge" belongs to an order of two-winged flies called *Diptera*, and those of interest to the fisherman usually are within the family *Chironomidae*. The *Chironomidae* have complete life cycles going from the egg, to the larva, to the pupa, and finally to the adult fly. Of the four stages, the middle two are probably most important to fly fishermen.

The larval stage of the *Chironomid* may be as small as one-eighth of an inch long and looks like a very slender worm or tube. These "worms" may float freely in the water and are taken readily by trout.

In the pupal stage, the insect develops an enlarged thorax, rudimentary wings which hang close to the underside of the abdomen and hairy gills which encircle the pupa behind the head. The pupae hang vertically with their gills in the surface film of the water and drift about until the adult "midge" hatches and flies away, leaving the empty pupal case behind.

The midge pupa.

It is the rise to the midge pupa which often proves to be our undoing. The trout actually takes the pupa in or just under the surface film, but his momentum or the force of his turn carries him slightly through the film, creating what appears to be the rise to a floating fly.

Adult midges may be seen flying in clouds over the water, but because they spend very little time *on* the water they are not as readily available to the fish as the earlier stage of the insect's life cycle.

Fishing the artificial midge pupa can be quite deadly and the fly will produce during the entire season. It is often stated in the literatures that the *Chironomidae* hatch from May to October. I, however, have observed trout eagerly feeding on the pupae in March and even earlier in the year during a snowstorm!

The midge pupa is very easy to tie, and no serious fly fisherman should be without a few in his fly box. The colors of the natural pupae range all the way from red to white. The most effective color that I've found has been a light gray, but it would be a good idea to match samples from your own stream. In the eastern United States, hook sizes run from 18 to 28, while in the West, some are tied on hooks as large as size 12 to 2X long.

The pupa is tied as follows: Begin with the tying silk placed on the hook at the bend and tie in a short piece of black tying silk to be used as a rib. Make a very thin body from the desired color of fur dubbing, ending about a quarter of the shank length behind the eye of the hook. The body should be only slightly larger in diameter than the hook itself. Next wind the rib in a counterclockwise direction, which will prevent it from disappearing into the fur dubbing (which should be wound clockwise). Ahead of the body tie in a piece of natural brown or gray ostrich herl; wrap two or three turns of herl around the hook, tie off, and the fly is finished.

The pupa should be fished upstream, dead drift, like a dry fly. I generally use at least a 6X leader tippet and often go to 7X if the fish are very particular. Since the natural pupa drifts in or just below the surface film, I usually grease the leader tippet down to within an inch of the fly, which will allow it to drift at the proper depth. On several occasions, however, I even have had to grease the ostrich herl collar of the fly (but not the body), so that it would float vertically in the surface film like the natural!

Another effective imitation may be made using a quill body and several turns of badger hackle for a collar. The badger fibers are then trimmed down to the dark center of the hackle.

Fishing the *Chironomid* pupa is "fine and fussy fishin'," but it just might be the solution to a very frustrating problem..."rising" trout that won't take a dry fly!

16.

Fifteen Ways to Improve Your Fly Tying

"Oh, you can tie all the fancy flies that you want, it's the ratty lookin' ones that catch the most fish." Have you heard that one before? I have, and almost invariably that is all that the speaker can tie...the ratty lookin' ones!

Now, I'll admit that occasionally a beat up old fly will take fish; I've had them keep hitting a fly until there was almost nothing left of it but the bare hook. But, for day after day results when the fishing is "fine an' fussy," give me a delicate, well tied bit of fluff any time.

Let's be honest about it. Do all of your flies look so real that your wife wants to swat them — or do they sometimes look as though she already had?

As a fly tying instructor and commercial fly tyer, I've had the opportunity to inspect thousands of flies and talk with many other tyers, and have come to the conclusion that most of us really could improve upon our creations. The "perfect" fly is as rare as a three pound brook trout, and, like the three pound brookie, is well worth searching for.

I have also found, when teaching my tying classes, that I tend to inject little bits of "philosophy" between the tying techniques. It finally occurred to me that I had been doing a little preaching along with the teaching. I jotted down a list of the points that I try to impress upon my students, and I suddenly realized that the proper mental approach to fly tying is very important if we are ever to tie that "perfect" fly.

I am convinced that we reach a point where our fly tying no longer improves because we stop thinking about what we are doing, and the process becomes merely routine mechanics. Unfortunately, this point is generally reached sometime before we come close to achieving "perfection."

With the hope that it will help experienced tyers improve their results and beginners to get off to a good start, here is my list of "Fifteen Ways To Improve Your Fly Tying." Many of you will already know and practice some of the items on the list, and some other items will seem quite obvious once you think about them. You will probably be able to think of other items of your own, and that's what this is really all about — we have to think about it if we are going to improve our fly tying.

1. *Use only the best tools and materials.* Only a few tools are required for fly tying, and the difference between the total cost for first quality and inferior tools may be only a few dollars. But, there is simply no way to place a value on the difference in performance between the two. You cannot tie a decent fly if your vise allows the hook to slip, your hackle pliers cause the hackle to break or slip, and the point of your scissors won't clip an individual hair. By the same token, you cannot tie a proper dry fly without top quality dry fly hackle.

Many beginners feel that it is best to start out with low quality tools and materials while they are "just learning." But, how can a beginner expect to learn to tie a high quality fly if an experienced tyer could not do a decent job using inferior tools and materials? Remember, it is more expensive to buy inadequate tools and later discard them than to buy the best initially.

2. *Use as fine a tying thread as possible.* Most tyers tend to use tying thread that is entirely too heavy. A finer thread will actually make a stronger, as well as a neater looking, fly. A fine thread allows one to take more turns around the material for added strength, but it does not build up unsightly bulk in the fly. Size 8/0 silk is certainly adequate for almost any dry fly and 6/0 is about right for most streamers. Several of my friends and I have gone so far as to unravel ladies nylon stockings to obtain the fine thread, and I now routinely use a thread called "Ultra-Midge" which mikes out to about 18-20/0.

A beginner often feels that he or she should use heavy thread so it won't break as often; but, beginners always break thread! It is better to learn to tie with the proper thread right from the start.

3. *Always tie a fly to the proper proportions and strive for uniformity.* Each style of fly has certain basic proportions which should be maintained relative to the hook size. For example, in most dry flies the tail should be the length of the hook shank, the hackle one and a half to two times the length of the gap of the hook, and the wings about one quarter longer than the hackle. The wings should be placed one quarter to one third of the length of the hook shank behind the eye. These proportions should be considered at each step of the tying process. An "expert's" flies will be consistently well proportioned and uniform whereas a beginner may well have a size 12 tail and hackle, and size 10 wings all on a size 14 hook!

4. *Always have a good background and adequate light at your tying bench.* Depending upon the materials being used, a piece of white or black paper beneath your vise will greatly improve the visual contrast and allow for a greater degree of precision in your work as well as prevent eye fatigue.

5. *Brush up on basic tying techniques.* It is very easy to get careless and try to take shortcuts that may detract from the quality of your finished fly. I often find that some of the best flies I tie are those I produce as demonstrations for a class. Why? Because I concentrate on doing each step properly and on using good basic techniques.

6. *Detect "problems" when they occur.* Why wait until the fly is finished to discover that the tail is too long? If you are critical of each step, errors can be corrected as they develop, and the finished fly will be greatly improved.

7. *The fly is not finished just because it is out of the vise.* Often the only difference between a good fly and an excellent one is a little judicious trimming after the fly is out of the vise. This does *not* mean to clip the wings, tail, or hackle to the proper length, but to look for stray hackle or tail fibers that protrude at odd angles, bits of dubbing that produce a lumpy body, or fibers caught under the thread windings of the head. Inspect each "finished" fly.

8. *Be very critical of each finished fly.* Ask yourself, "What is wrong with this fly?" Compare it with a fly tied by an experienced tyer, and ask for criticism from others. How can you improve your next fly if you don't know what was wrong with the last one?

9. *Watch others tie and ask all of the questions you can.* Books are very helpful, but there is no substitute for watching an experienced tyer. Almost always the better tyers will be more than happy to help you in any way that they can, but you must go to them; don't expect them to offer advice until asked.

10. *Join a fly tying club or start one yourself.* No matter where you live, you should be able to find others who are interested in fly tying or fishing. Even a loosely organized group can promote an interchange of ideas and techniques that are certain to help each member improve his or her fly tying ability.

11. *There are few right or wrong fly tying methods.* There are many different techniques for achieving the same end result. Therefore, don't have a closed mind; learn as many new methods as you can, and use the ones that work best for you.

12. *Experiment with new techniques and study the insects you want to imitate.* You will usually find that the best fly tyers are not content to do things in the "old way." They constantly look for new ways to improve their flies, new materials to use, and better imitations for specific insects.

13. *Don't worry about tying speed.* It is better to produce one perfect fly in thirty minutes than a dozen poor flies in the same length of time. When I tie, I'm often asked, "How can you tie so quickly?" My answer is, "Don't worry about speed!" As your tying improves you will learn the little tricks that lead to faster tying, but first concentrate on quality.

14. *Don't be satisfied with "good enough."* "Good enough" may catch fish, but your tying will never improve if you settle for anything less than your very best. You must constantly try to make each fly better than the previous one.

15. *Practice!* Finally, as in most endeavors, improvement only comes with thoughtful practice. Tie as often as you can and make a conscious effort to improve your results. Then one day you will look at

last year's flies and think, "My gosh, did I tie those ratty looking things?" By then you'll be well on your way to gaining a reputation as a fly tying "expert."

Good luck!

17.

Tips for the Tyer

I don't know if all fly tyers are like me or not, but if seems that my life at the tying bench is one constant series of problems. Not big, catastrophic problems, but little nagging problems that make life irritating.

I go along grumbling at the irritations until finally I can't stand them any longer, and then out of desperation, I set out to find a solution to the problem. Or, I'll say, "Why the heck didn't I think of that a long time ago!"

But, just as I solve one problem, a couple more jump up at me and I bumble ever onward.

Over the years, though, I have managed to solve a few problems that other tyers might share, and perhaps I shouldn't keep the good news to myself.

For example, I was always irritated by head cement. Plain old head cement! If the top is left off the bottle while tying, the stuff soon becomes too thick to use. But, it's such a nuisance to keep screwing the cap off and on every time a single drop is needed. If several dozen flies are tied, the time used just opening and closing the bottle really adds up. A small problem but irritating.

The solution came while working in my laboratory—a chemical bottle called a "balsam bottle" with a ground glass cap! Suddenly, using the head cement was no problem at all. The dubbing needle is held between the thumb and index finger of the right hand, while the cap is removed from the bottle in the crook of the little finger. As soon as the drop of cement is picked up by the needle, the cap is replaced by merely dropping it back in place. A thin film of silicone stopcock grease around the ground glass rim of the cap maintains an air seal to prevent the cement from thickening in the bottle. That's it, no muss, no fuss.

Balsam bottles should be available through most drug stores, although a special order may have to be placed. You might also try your friendly dentist the next time you go in for a check up. Either way, I would suggest getting the smallest bottle of this type that you can find.

I guess by now most tyers have discovered the kitchen blender for mixing dubbing. I wonder how many have also discovered the problem of static electricity which, in the winter or in dry climates, causes the spun fur to stick tenaciously to the side and top of the blender, your hands, and everything else with which it comes into contact? I thought this one would be quite easily solved, and I felt rather smug as I went down to the laundry room to look for the anti-static stuff my wife sprays into the drier. But, no such luck. After spraying the inside of the blender all I had was a tacky, matted clump of useless dubbing. While I have since heard of other tyers using this agent, none of the brands I tried worked well at all. So back to the old drawing board.

This time the light dawned as I was cleaning a stack of records for the stereo. I never did hear the records, but dashed up to the tying room to try the record cleaning solution inside the blender. I sprinkled a few drops of the solution on a small cloth pad, and wiped it over the inside surface of the blending jar and lid, threw in a batch of fur, and presto! Perfectly blended dubbing, and *no static electricity*!

The stuff I used is called "discwasher," but I'm sure any similar product will work as well. Once treated, the blender will repel the static electricity build up for several batches of dubbing. When I see it starting to build up again, another wiping with the solution eliminates the problem. One word of caution, though. If your blender is also used in the kitchen, make sure it is washed extra carefully after using the record cleaning solution. The stuff is toxic when taken internally. Incidentally, that problem can be solved by purchasing of the small electric coffee grinders to use as a mini-blender strictly in the tying room.

Since this article was originally written, I have also discovered that the anti-static papers such as Bounce that are placed into a clothes dryer also work very well for removing static electricity from both hands and blenders.

Another problem which arose as a result of the dry air here in Idaho where I live is dry fingers. More specifically, a dry tip on my thumb and index finger which sometimes makes it difficult to spin fur dubbing directly onto the tying silk. Instead of spinning nicely onto the thread, the fur just lays there while my fingers slide on by. Hand lotion was only a very temporary solution at best, and I soon found myself moistening my finger tips in my mouth. That is, until I realized that the raw furs I was handling were even dirtier than my own fingers.

This time the solution to the problem was found while watching a bank teller count a stack of greenbacks. First she dipped her fingers into a little plastic box which contained — you guessed it — Magic Touch Finger Moistener. This, or similar material, is available in any stationery or office supply shop, and it's done wonders for my temper and the status of my health. No more fingers in the mouth; just touch them to the surface of the finger moistener, rub it in a bit, and spin away!

Of course, every tyer keeps a small square of ultra fine sandpaper handy to smooth out rough spots of skin on the fingers that snag the tying silk. Don't they? A 400 grit wet or dry finishing paper is perfect (No, I didn't get this one from watching a safecracker at work).

Do you ever have problems finding just the right hair to make a good stiff dry fly tail? You know the kind, it's as stiff as wire, doesn't flare out all over the place when you tie it in, and a few fibers will support a dry fly perfectly. It doesn't have to be a problem any longer if you can obtain the scent pads from the hind legs of a buck deer. These pads are usually the first thing a successful hunter cuts off and discards before field dressing a deer. But, what a waste! Place them in a small plastic sandwich bag and take them home. A good washing will clean them up nicely, and they'll give you hair for many, many perfect dry fly tails. If you don't hunt, you'd better pass out a few sandwich bags to your hunting friends. A few bags are a good investment. And, if you haven't tried hair tails on some of your standard patterns, you'll be amazed at how well they help the fly to float.

How many times have you fumbled around in the middle of the stream with a stubborn can of dry fly grease? The top sticks, or is too greasy to grip, or it has melted all over the inside of your vest pocket and thoroughly saturated all of your wet flies and nymphs, which will never sink again. And the process always requires one hand for the rod, one hand for the fly, one hand for the lid, and one hand to grease the fly.

There are a number of solutions to this problem, but the one that works the best for me is simplicity in itself. Wrap a snake guide onto an empty lip salve tube and clip the tube to one of the button sized pin-on chain retrievers. Fill the tube with your favorite grease, pin it to your vest and you're all set. When the grease is needed, remove the cap with the crook of your little finger, place a dab of grease on your index finger, and replace the cap. Release the tube and the chain will be pulled back into place and out of the way. Neat!

Next, a very sticky problem. I rarely use wax when tying flies, as my method works quite well without it. But, when a situation does arise which requires wax, I want it *sticky*. Invariably my old unused wax is dry and hard, and completely unusable when it's finally needed, and it wasn't sticky enough in the first place.

The solution to this one came while I was waxing my touring skis before taking the family on a cross-country ski tour. The perfect *sticky* tying wax turned out to be the soft cross-country ski wax that is used for wet spring snow. Not the kind called klister that comes in tubes, but the softest kind that is sold in small lead foil cylinders. Swix or Rex brands of yellow wax are perfect, or tell your dealer that you want the wax that is used for wet snow when the temperature is just above freezing. But remember, the stuff is *sticky*, and a little goes a long way. Peel back a little of the foil container to expose the wax and *very gently* run it along your tying silk. It may take a bit of experimenting to get just the right amount, but when you do you will have a thread that is waxed! And, yes, Virginia, the stuff really does make skis slide — you figure it out.

Now for one last trick that will illustrate the use of the above wax, and, at the same time, demonstrate a way to tie very shaggy nymph bodies. While I prefer nymphs with nice fuzzy bodies such as those dubbed with fur that has the guard hairs left in, I used to do my best to avoid having to tie them. I know there are a variety of methods for tying this type of body, but none of them seemed to be right for me. Some took too long, some produced a loose body, some weren't shaggy enough, and none of them gave me the control of the final product that I desired. That is, it was difficult to control the taper or shape of the body.

The solution to the problem came in two stages. The first was when someone showed me a simple little twisting tool made from a bent paper clip, and the second when I adapted the use of the very sticky cross-country ski wax. Once the trick was perfected, I began to turn out fuzzy bodied nymphs with a vengeance. They were quick to produce, tightly wrapped, very fuzzy, and I found that I had excellent control of all aspects of the finished fly.

The ingenious little twisting tool is made by straightening out a paper clip, and then bending a small hook onto one end of it. As originally conceived, this tool was used to form a loop in the tying thread into which the dubbing fur was to be placed and twisted together.

My fuzzy bodies improved somewhat after I discovered the paper clip twister, but I still had a problem placing the fur evenly into the loop of tying silk or distributing it the way I wanted it. Then I discovered the ski wax. The tying process is now as follows.

After placing the fly hook into the vise, secure the tying silk near the bend and tie in the required tail material. When the tail is secure, wind the silk back to the most rearward point of the body and pull off four inches or so of silk from the bobbin. Wax this section of silk with the ski wax. Hold the bobbin in your left hand with the waxed tying silk pulled away from the hook toward you.

The fur dubbing can now be distributed evenly along the length of the waxed silk, or, if a tapered body is desired, place a small amount of fur close to the hook and add larger amounts as you progress down the silk toward the bobbin. You will find that the fur can almost be dropped into place without your fingers even touching the waxed tying silk. The trick is to not mat the dubbing down onto the silk, but let it lay loosely on the thread. The very sticky ski wax will hold it in place.

Now switch the bobbin to your right hand and pick up the twisting tool in your left. The tool is "loaded" by taking a loop of bare, unwaxed tying silk from the bobbin around the paper clip hook. With the tool loaded, pass the silk from the bobbin over the dubbed silk and back to the exact point on the hook where the dubbed silk is secured. Fasten the bare silk to the hook at this point with a few turns around the shank. The result will be a closed loop of tying silk with the tool holding the bottom of the loop, and the dubbing distributed between the strands. Wind the tying silk forward to the point where the body will end.

Let the bobbin hang below the hook at this point and transfer the twisting tool to the right hand. Grasp the leg of the tool between the index finger and thumb, and spin it rapidly in a clockwise direction. This will cause the two strands of the loop to twist and produce a tight fur rope.

When the rope is spun as tightly as possible without breaking the thread, grip the end of the loop just ahead of the twisting tool with a hackle pliers and slip the tool off the loop. Apply a few drops of head cement to the shank of the hook, and wrap the fur rope onto the hook as you would a strand of wool or chenille. The fur can also be wrapped by holding the tool itself rather than using a hackle pliers, whichever is most convenient.

When the fur is wrapped to the forward position of the body, tie it off with the tying silk, which was left hanging at that point, and complete the fly as usual.

You will find that this technique will allow you to control many aspects of the fuzzy body that were previously left mainly to chance. If an even shaggier body is desired, merely clip more guard hairs into the dubbing during the blending process. If a very thin body is required, as in a damsel fly nymph, just use a small amount of dubbing over the entire length of the loop. Or, if a fat body is desired, use a larger amount of dubbing over the entire length of the loop.

Incidentally, a dubbed body can be roughed up even more by stroking it with a short piece of an old hacksaw blade.

So there you have it. My solutions to a few of the problems that have bugged me over the years. I hope they will work as well for you and will stimulate you to try to solve some of your own problems in a thoughtful way.

18.

How to Make a Mottled Turkey Quill

At first glance, there doesn't appear to be anything too unusual about the photo of a Dave's Hopper. In fact, you can inspect the picture closely and still not find anything out of the ordinary. It seems to be a perfectly normal fly, until you're told that the fly's wing is *not* a mottled turkey quill!

Because most domestic turkeys raised for the table are now white, the supply of traditional "oak" or mottled wing feathers required by many popular fly patterns has decreased steadily. High quality feathers for the wings of such flies as the Muddler Minnow, Joe's Hopper, Dave's Hopper, and various caddis imitations have become more difficult and expensive to obtain in recent years.

Now, thanks to modern technology, I believe the problem can be solved. The wing of the pictured hopper started life as a white goose feather and was transformed into a turkey quill by felt-tipped pens and India ink.

A trip to your local pharmacy, stationery shop or artist's supply house will produce a wide variety of felt-tipped pens in suitable shades of brown. Any brand of *waterproof* pen will work, but if you happen to find Prismacolor pens, you've hit the jackpot. These artist's pens are available in dozens of shades. The Prismacolor pens that I have found useful in producing turkey quills are color nos. 8941, 8944 and 8946. If you want to save a little money, just a couple of these pens or another brand of waterproof marker will do a fine job. Be sure to test the colors on a piece of paper to pick the shades you like and to buy the broad chisel point pens rather than the sharply pointed ones.

In addition to the pens, a real turkey feather is useful as a model, and you'll need a small bottle of brown waterproof India ink. I use Pelikan no. 15 (sepia).

I begin by giving the good side of the white goose quill a light pinkish-tan cast with a coat of Prismacolor no. 8939 (flesh). This color is best applied by laying the feather on a piece of paper and brushing the quill firmly with the pen. Apply the color in streaks and patches, leaving some areas uncolored. If you use a brand other than Prismacolor, the flesh shade can be omitted, and you can begin with the next step.

The white goose quill is first mottled with several shades of brown marking pen.

After mottling with the marking pens, the goose quill is spatter painted with brown waterproof India ink and a toothbrush. Disposable plastic gloves can be worn to protect the hands.

Dave's Hopper with turkey quill made from a white goose quill.

Using a darker shade of brown, Prismacolor no. 8941, for example, brush on the primary turkey color. If the feather is held flat on a paper and the pen is pressed firmly, the feather will take on a dense, dark color. If you hold the feather in the air and gently stroke it with the pen, a lighter, more broken hue is obtained. Try both methods and experiment with the effects that they produce. Remember, this is to be a *mottled* feather; so apply the color in streaks and splotches.

After the basic color has been applied, you can either proceed to the final step or touch up the feather with other shades, such as the dark Prismacolor no. 8946 or the rusty-brown no. 8944. When you are satisfied with the basic appearance of your quill, go on to the final step.

At this point, the feather still doesn't look much like the desired turkey quill, for the transformation occurs in the last step. Brown India ink, a small paper cup, an old toothbrush, a rubber glove and some newspaper are needed for this operation.

Lay the painted feather on the newspaper and pour a small amount of ink into the paper cup. Dip the toothbrush into the ink and run a rubber gloved finger over the bristles to spatter the ink onto the feather. Hold the brush with the bristles facing downward and stroke from the bottom. Keep spattering until you're satisfied with the appearance of the quill.

When the feather is completely dry, I like to spray it with a light coat of Grumbacher's Tuffilm. This gives the fibers strength and durability. The spray, a handy item at the tying bench, is available from most art supply dealers.

When placed side-by-side with a natural turkey feather, your artificial still will not likely be confused with the real thing. But when a small section of the man-made feather is tied into a fly, it is very difficult, if not impossible, to tell that it hasn't come from a real turkey.

19.

Scuds

f I had to choose one type of fishing with which to occupy the rest of my days, there would be no doubt that it would be trout fishing on a cool, clear limestone spring creek with an occasional venture to a lake filled with the same type of water. Such alkaline waters are rich in insect life. The trout in them grow fat and strong, and they often prove to be the ultimate angling challenge.

Should I be fortunate enough to be consigned to such idyllic waters, my fly box would have to contain a broad assortment of scuds. Often called "fresh water shrimp," these crustaceans are usually found in tremendous numbers in rich, alkaline spring water, and trout love 'em.

Ranging in size from under a half inch in length to well over an inch, these little creatures actively swim and drift about the tops of the weed beds and make easy pickings for the trout. At times, mass "drifts" of the scuds occur in spring creeks as thousands upon thousands of them let the current carry them downstream. At such times, the fishing can be almost beyond belief.

Anglers who regularly fish spring fed lakes or streams are missing a good bet if they don't carry a large supply of scud patterns. A number of patterns are effective, and they range from simple fur dubbed creations to more highly involved ties. The pattern which I generally prefer takes a middle-of-the-road approach. Simple to tie, it is, at the same time, quite realistic, and best of all, it has produced extremely well for me.

A hook of the appropriate size to match the naturals is first bent to a *very slight* "hump-backed" curve, and weighted with fuse wire. Don't overdo the curve, since the scuds swim in an essentially straight position.

Tie in a rib of dark grey buttonhole thread (or finer thread for the smaller flies) near the bend of the hook, and follow this by tying in a narrow strip of grey Swiss Straw or clear plastic bag material at the same point the rib was tied in. Then, secure a medium blue dun hackle by the butt of its stem near the bend of the hook just ahead of the materials previously tied in. Dub a soft fur under-body over the length of the hook shank. Colors range from grey, to olive, to pinkish olive, to dirty yellow, to tan.

Naturals can easily be caught by pulling up a small clump of weeds

The Scud.

from the bottom—you'll probably be amazed at the number you'll find. Look at their body colors and try to match them with your artificials.

After dubbing the under-body, palmer the hackle forward over the entire length of the hook and tie it off. Fold the Swiss Straw forward over the back and sides of the under-body. This step should cause the hackles to fold down and project under the fly to form the legs. Tie off the shell, and rib with the thread previously tied in at the bend of the hook.

Finish off the fly with a rather large head, and pull several of the leg fibers forward from the head to form antennae.

Since scuds often swim backwards, some fly tyers like to reverse the fly on the hook in some of their imitations. But the little critters swim both forward and backwards, as well as on their sides and upside down, so I generally just tie them in the manner described.

The techniques for fishing the scuds are quite straightforward. The most important consideration is to be certain that the fly has reached the proper depth before beginning your retrieve—just about even with the tops of the weeds. Often this can best be accomplished with the "count-down technique." Start a count as the fly hits the water, and wait until you think it has reached the right depth. If the fly fails to tick the weeds occasionally on the retrieve, count a little longer before retrieving your next cast.

Since the scuds are active swimmers, a variety of retrieves can be effective—try a slow hand-twist technique, or give the fly erratic little strips, let it sink, and twitch it again. In moving water, a dead drift can often be effective. The key is to experiment, after being certain that the fly is at the correct depth. When you've got it right, the trout will let you know immediately!

SCUD PATTERN

HOOK: 18-8, 1-3XL to match the natural (Bent to slight curve and weighted)

THREAD: Grey

SHELL: Grey Swiss Straw or clear plastic bag material

RIB: Dark grey buttonhole thread (finer thread for smallest flies)

UNDER-BODY: Fur the color of naturals (olive, grey, pink/olive, dirty yellow, tan)

HACKLE (Legs): Medium blue dun, palmered over under-body and folded down by the shell

HEAD: Large with a few hackle fibers pulled forward from the top to form antennae

20.

The Marabou Swimming Nymph

Next to fishing a perky dry fly for freely rising trout, I like nymph fishing. It has almost become an angling cliché to say that the vast majority of the time trout feed on underwater life forms rather than on surface flies, and the expert nymph fisherman will often score where others fail. But, it's true; nymph fishing can be deadly.

However, in addition to providing me with many pleasant hours on the stream, my fascination with nymphs has been the cause of a great deal of frustration at the tying bench. Now, don't get me wrong; I enjoy tying nymphs and feel that I can do a fair to middlin' job of tying imitations that *look* reasonably like the naturals. The frustration comes when I realize that these great looking little bugs probably don't *act* anything at all like the naturals when I fish them. To be sure, I do catch fish on my nymphs so they probably are not too bad, but I know that something is missing.

Have you ever watched a nymph swimming in a stream or lake? I have, and the fact that impressed me most was how active the little dickens are. Their long bodies are constantly wiggling up and down in a vigorous motion, which propels the insect through the water. Rarely do you see a nymph that has no motion at all.

Fly tyers have tried a variety of methods to give the illusion of life to their nymphs. Most commonly, soft furs and feathers are used, which can easily be moved by the current or rod action to add "life" to the fly. It is generally considered best to sacrifice some realism in the appearance of the artificial nymph in order to gain this lifelike motion of the materials. The lack of life probably explains why molded plastic nymphs, which are exact replicas of naturals, are usually very much inferior to less accurate representations when it comes to catching fish.

Thus, our patterns are on the right track, but I have always felt that there had to be some way to make our artificials act still more lifelike; that is, some way to put in the wiggle.

The answer finally came to me, and when it did it was so simple that it was hard to realize that no one had thought of it before! The answer came in a roundabout way, as is usual with the solutions to long-standing problems. This one came from watching a streamer

Marabou Swimming Nymph with free style wing case.

Marabou Swimming Nymph with down style wing case.

fisherman. The late Ben Egger, of the St. Paul (Minnesota) Fly Fisher-man's Club, was one of the best streamer fishermen that I've ever met. Ben specialized in stalking big fish, and his season record for trout of over three pounds would be the envy of anyone. He did it in the Midwest where large trout are not too commonplace, and he did it with streamer flies of his own design.

Ben's success was the result of many factors, but especially how he tied his streamers, and how he fished them. He used the longest and softest marabou fibers that he could find, and tied them on rather short streamer hooks, which were weighted only near the head of the fly. As a result, his flies dart, dive, twitch, and wiggle like no other streamer I've ever seen. When the tension on the leader is eased, the fly goes into a headfirst dive and when the leader is tightened the fly climbs toward the surface. By twitching the rod tip during the retrieve, the fly can be made to dance and unduluate like a go-go girl gone wild.

After years of watching Ben fish his marabou streamers, I realized I had my answer for a more lifelike acting nymph.

The day the light finally dawned, I tied a few experimental models and rushed to try them in my white, porcelain fly testing tank (my family calls it the bathroom sink). It was exactly what I had been look-ing for! The results were later verified by a panel of experts — a brawl-ing bunch of fifteen and sixteen inch rainbows that practically knocked the feathers off the nymphs the first time I tried them.

As can be seen in the accompanying photographs, the nymphs are tied with an extended body of marabou. Since only the thorax, legs and covert are tied directly to the hook, the hooks used are undersized for the size of the fly being tied. For example a size 12 hook will produce a fly of the size normally tied on a size 6 or 8 hook. When tying small nymphs, select a hook with a 3-4X short shank. This will allow for a short fly without sacrificing the bite of the hook.

I tie the nymphs in two different styles—one with a shell type covert and one with a free-style covert. Colors are dependent upon the species being imitated. I use brown, black, olive, and gray.

The first several steps are the same for either style covert. Wrap the shank of the hook with tying silk to a point just above the barb of the hook. Place a few drops of head cement on the hook and wrap the shank with lead wire. The hook must be very heavily weighted to produce the desired action. It must dive headfirst when pressure is released from the leader. Therefore, use a heavy gauge of lead wire, or double wrap the hook with lighter wire.

The extended body is made from marabou fibers. Tie in a long clump of brown marabou just above the barb of the hook so the feathers extend back from the bend like a fluffy tail. Do not use too large a clump of marabou, as this will destroy the action of the fibers. A two-toned body can be produced if desired by tying a clump of dark marabou over a small clump of light colored marabou. Once the marabou is tied in, cut it off at the length appropriate to the size fly being tied.

If a shell style covert is being tied, proceed as follows. Cut a section of fibers about one-quarter inch wide from a brown duck or goose flight quill and bind it to the hook shank at a point just above the barb of the hook. Tie it in so that it lies flat on the hook and projects backward over the body. At the same point, tie in a soft brown wet fly hackle and two peacock herl.

Wrap the peacock herl around the weighted hook shank to form the thorax. Palmer the hackle forward over the thorax and tie it off. Clip off the hackle from the top and bottom of the thorax so that the only fibers remaining project out from the sides of the thorax.

Bend the quill section forward over the thorax and tie it down ahead of the thorax. Don't clip off the excess quill at this time, but form the head of the nymph with tying silk and complete with a whip finish. With a dubbing needle separate one fiber from each side of the excess quill section. Cut off the portion of the quill between these two fibers, and trim the remaining fibers to length as antennae.

To tie the nymph with the free-style covert rather than the shell type, weight the hook and tie in the marabou body as before. Do not tie in the flight quill section or the hackle, but simply tie in and wind on the peacock herl thorax. After tying down the herl fibers at the front of the thorax, bind on a section of wing quill so that it protrudes back over the thorax. Trim the back edge of the quill section to a V shape and trim the antennae as before. An effective free-style covert can also be made from a short tuft of the same marabou that was used to form the nymph's body. Tie in wisps of bronze mallard flank on either side of the head to form the legs of the nymph; form the head and the fly is completed.

The marabou swimming nymph style of tying produces by far the most effective damsel fly nymph imitation that I have ever used, and by tying it all black in large sizes it is an excellent leech pattern.

Before you fish these nymphs observe them in the water and practice twitching the rod tip to make the flies wiggle like the natural. The fly can be fished as you would fish any other nymph, but the secret is to make it swim by giving it action with the rod tip. Just don't overdo it; a light twitching action is all that is needed.

But, a word of warning! After you make your first cast, hang on to your hat — the trout really sock these swimming nymphs.

21.

The Day and Night Nymphs

B ack in the sixties the Orvis company marketed a six fly, two pattern set of my flies under the cryptic name "The Day and Night Series." As I recall, these two patterns were the first flies of my own design that ever achieved some measure of popularity with other anglers.

Prior to the time I moved to Pennsylvania in the mid-sixties, I had been struggling to learn the mysterious art of fly tying entirely on my own. I read what I could find on the subject, experimented a little, and turned out horrible creations of which I was unjustly proud. I had seen only one other person actually tie a fly, but since he was almost as new to the art as I, he was of little help.

Then, shortly after moving to Pennsylvania, I met George Harvey. I hounded George with questions almost daily, watched him at his vise by the hour, and finally it all started to come together for me. Thanks to George, my flies began to look like proper flies.

One of the unusual aspects of George's flies, in addition to their perfection, was the colors of their bodies. They were not at all the monochromatic colors normally seen at that time, but rather were subtle shades with nebulous flecks of color showing through, and when wet, they almost magically took on an incredible translucency.

George's secret, as I was to learn, was that the bodies were blended from several different colors of fur to produce the ultimate subtle shades. Today, of course, such blending is the norm for fly tyers everywhere, but in those days it was a revolutionary technique. George had been doing it for years, though, and as far as I know, he was among the first to develop the technique.

It was while I was playing with my newly learned fur blending technique that I combined a very bright orange rabbit fur with medium yellow and white furs to inadvertently produce the dubbing for the fly that was to ultimately become the "Day" component of the Day and Night Series. The resulting combination of furs was a soft sulfur–orange color which I originally produced for a dry version of the Pale Sulfur — *E. dorothea*.

One day, on a whim, I tied a nymph pattern with the material and thought the result to be quite attractive. Apparently the trout thought so too, because the nymph proved to be extremely effective when used in our local waters. In fact, it soon became one of my favorites, and when I shared a few with friends they agreed — they did very well with them.

The fly, while tied in the traditional nymph style, was not meant to represent a particular species, but was merely a "nymph." The only difference between it and hundreds of other patterns was in the dubbing. When wet, the white in the blend disappeared, the orange became more prominent, and the body seemed to swell and assume a very "juicy" translucent appearance. It looked like something that just had to be sampled by the trout.

The importance of this blend was discovered by one friend, Blake Anderson, who attempted to tie some of the nymphs for himself using a monochromatic orange angora fur yarn for dubbing. When dry the angora looked virtually identical in color to the blend, but upon wetting there was no comparison — the angora looked flat and dead, while the blend became alive. In stream tests the difference between the two body materials was equally distinct.

The new fly was still without a name when one day, while watching me tie a few of them, my young son, Eric, picked up a ball of the dubbing and exclaimed, "It looks like orange juice!" Thus, the fly was christened the "O.J. Nymph."

After using the O.J. for a season or two, I happened to be fishing with Dick Finlay, then of the Orvis Company, and I gave a few to him and asked him to try them in his travels around the country. By the time our paths crossed again, Dick was an enthusiastic believer. He reported that they had worked very well wherever he had used them, but he was desperate! He'd lost his last one, and did I have any more he could take with him? I did, and he did.

Any normal nymphing technique can be used in fishing the O.J.; the secret to its success is in the dubbing, not the fishing method. We did discover, however, that *when* you use the fly is important. After using the O.J. for some time, it became apparent that there were certain conditions under which it was considerably more effective than others.

It seemed to catch many more fish when the water was clear rather than cloudy, and it seemed to work better when the sun was on the water than when the day was dark or in the evening. Our conclusion was that the clear water and sunshine enhanced the illusion of translucency in the body of the fly. In off color water, the fly was simply not as visible to the fish.

After some consideration of the fact that I seemed to have created a clear water, daytime fly, I decided that a general nymph pattern for the opposite conditions was in order. There were, of course, many patterns already in existence which would meet this need, but I wanted to develop my own pattern as a partner for the O.J. A "matched set" so to speak.

As most of us know, a dark fly is much more visible to the fish in discolored water or in the evening when there is little sunlight on the water. The opaqueness of the fly helps it to be seen by the fish.

Therefore, my "night" nymph was created from all black materials with the exception of a wing case of wood duck flank feather for aesthetics and a gold wire rib that would tend to pick up and reflect what little light might be available. Again, the fly was tied and fished in typical nymph fashion.

Sometimes, the naming of a new fly pattern is a simple matter brought on by special circumstances, while in other cases appropriately naming an original creation is the very difficult result of a conscious effort to do so. In this case, the name was easy. I called it the Styx River Nymph after the mythical Greek river of darkness which bounds the gates to Hades.

I included a few of the Styx patterns in the next box of O.J.s, which I sent to Dick Finlay, and he, along with other friends with whom I'd shared them, soon confirmed that the new pattern did work very well under the conditions for which it was designed—discolored water or evening fishing. It also was Dick, I believe, who suggested that the O.J. and the Styx be called the "Day and Night Series."

Ultimately, at Dick's suggestion, I began to tie the nymphs for inclusion in the Orvis catalog, and the tying of hundreds of dozens of the patterns helped to support me as a graduate student at Penn State. While I have long since stopped tying flies commercially, both of these patterns have retained a place in my fly box. Since leaving Pennsylvania, I have been lucky enough to have had opportunities to fish in many parts of the world, and both the O.J. and the Styx River Nymphs have remained very effective when used under the conditions for which they were designed.

THE O.J. NYMPH

HOOK: Mustad 9671-2XL or 7957B, sizes 12-16, weighted or not as desired

THREAD: Brown

TAILS: Wood duck flank feather fibers, tied sparse

RIB: Brown tying thread (Size A)

BODY: Blend of rabbit furs; one-third bright orange, one-third medium yellow, and one-third white

WING CASE: Brown dyed duck quill section tied "down" style. After tying off at head, leave two short quill fibers as antennae

THORAX: Dark Brown fur dubbing

LEGS: Brown hackle palmered over thorax, and clipped off top and bottom to leave legs only at sides of thorax

THE STYX RIVER NYMPH

> HOOK: Mustad 9671-2XL or 7957B, Sizes 12-16, weighted or not as desired
>
> THREAD: Black
>
> TAILS: Small clump of black hackle fibers
>
> RIB: Fine gold wire
>
> BODY: Black dyed rabbit fur
>
> WING CASE: Wood duck flank feather fibers tied "down" style
>
> THORAX: Black dyed rabbit fur
>
> LEGS: Black hackle palmered over thorax and clipped off top and bottom to leave legs only at the sides.

22.

The Joe Brooks
Memorial Flies

J oe Brooks is gone. The word came in late September, 1972, in a
phone call from a mutual friend.

We had known that Joe's heart was not good, but he had been taking it a little easier, relaxing a bit more now, and he looked great. I had
fished with him earlier that summer, and my wife and I had spent a
few pleasant hours with him and his wife Mary in Livingston only a
month ago. Now he was gone.

Joe Brooks. What fly fisherman does not know the name? Here was
a giant among men. A man who fished with princes, with kings, with
the most famous fishermen the world over — and with everyday anglers
like you and me whom he met on every stream he fished.

Like most of us, I'd read Joe's fishing stories as a boy. I had felt,
through his pen, the delicate take of a brown trout to a tiny dry fly,
and the powerful surge of a mighty British Columbia steelhead. He had
made my dreams come alive with his words.

It was many years later that I first met Joe and his charming wife,
Mary. I was in awe of that first meeting, knowing that I had a date to
fish with Joe Brooks. But of course, I needn't have worried. It was like
being on the stream with an old friend, for that was what Joe soon
became to everyone he met. Joe was many things to many people, but
above all, Joe Brooks was a gentleman.

He's gone now, but through his work and his writing, he will live
on in the hearts of fishermen wherever a dry fly dances on sparkling
water.

I sat alone in my den after I received word of his passing. It took a
couple of hours to find the right words to put into a sympathy note to
Mary. Then I just sat there and thought about fishing, and Joe.

My fly-tying vise stood empty, and I thought about the many flies
that Joe had discussed in his writing. Then it occurred to me — was
there no fly that bore Joe Brooks' name? Yes, I knew of the Blonde
series that he had developed, but was there no Joe Brooks fly? I checked
several references, but could find nothing.

I picked up a sketch pad and began to doodle. What would a proper Joe Brooks fly look like? I had often designed flies to match various

insects, but never before set out to tie a memorial to a man.

It could not be a garishly bright fly; it would have to be a "gentleman fly," like Joe, at home anywhere.

There was no question about the hackle. If you had ever seen Joe without his hat, you knew that the hackle had to be grizzly gray. The wings? Joe always liked white hair wings; that would do nicely. The tail would be grizzly to match the hackle.

The body posed a problem. It had to present a buggy appearance in order to catch fish. Above all else, Joe's fly had to catch fish. Since this fly was not to match a specific insect, it must match many insects. The answer seemed clear. The body must be of blended fur dubbing. But what shade?

Perhaps a bit of tan; Joe's face was always burnished by the sun. And orange and yellow for the sunsets that he loved so much. A touch of olive that exists in so many mayflies, and a little white to give the fly translucency when wet. What would it all look like? I blended a small batch of the proper colored rabbit furs and the result seemed perfect. The subtle hints of color formed an ideal blend to give the body character. And Joe's eyes always had a sparkle. The fly would have to have a silver rib.

These materials would make a dry fly, and a steelhead–salmon fly. A streamer fly would require a little more trim.

Peacock herl strands would represent the lateral line of a small bait-fish and white bucktail its belly. The wings would be grizzly with a topping of the crest of the golden pheasant; Joe certainly should have a golden crown. The cheeks would be elegant silver pheasant; Joe was always elegant. Finally there had to be the rare jungle cock feather. Joe was, indeed, a rare person, and was a founder of the Order of the Jungle Cock, an organization dedicated to helping young boys learn fly fishing.

On paper, the flies looked good, but the final judgment would have to be made on the finished product. A few minutes time produced a dry, a wet, a steelhead–salmon fly and a streamer.

I studied them from every angle. The colors blended together very well, and the overall appearance was exactly what I had sought. There was no question that they would catch fish. I was pleased.

I suppose one should not sit down at the vise with the intention of "creating a great fly." Time and fish-catching ability should be the factors that lead to greatness. But these flies are for a man; a great man. Perhaps time will prove them deserving of their name. I hope so. I think Joe would have liked them.

JOE BROOKS DRY FLY

> HACKLE:Grizzly
>
> WING:White calf tail
>
> BODY:Blend of tan, orange, yellow, olive, and white rabbit fur to produce a rusty brown shade
>
> RIB:Fine silver wire
>
> TAIL:Grizzly hackle fibers
>
> SILK:Herb Howard or Danville's pre-waxed orange

JOE BROOKS WET FLY

> HACKLE:Grizzly, tied beard style
>
> WING:White calf, tied down-wing style
>
> BODY:Blended rabbit furs, as in dry fly
>
> RIB:Medium oval or fine flat silver tinsel
>
> TAIL:Grizzly hackle fibers
>
> SILK:Herb Howard or Danville's pre-waxed orange

JOE BROOKS STEELHEAD–SALMON FLY

> HACKLE:Grizzly, tied in as a collar under the wing
>
> WING:White calf tail, tied in down wing style over the hackle collar
>
> BODY:Blended fur dubbing as in dry fly
>
> RIB:Wide oval or medium flat silver tinsel
>
> TAG: Silver to match ribbing
>
> TAIL:None
>
> SILK: Herb Howard or Danville's pre-waxed orange

JOE BROOKS STREAMER FLY

> BODY:Blended fur as in dry fly
>
> RIB:Oval silver tinsel
>
> TAG:Oval silver tinsel
>
> BELLY:Small bunch of white bucktail under four peacock herl
>
> WING:Four grizzly hackle feathers matched in pairs with concave sides facing
>
> TOPPING: Crest feather from a golden pheasant
>
> CHEEKS:Silver pheasant
>
> EYES:Jungle cock
>
> SILK:Herb Howard or Danville's pre-waxed orange

23.

Custom Built Fly Rods—
The Search for Perfection

It's happened to me, and if you've done very much shopping for fly rods, it's probably happened to you, too. You find a rod with the action you like, but the grip doesn't feel quite right. Or maybe you don't care for the reel seat. Or you prefer larger guides, more of them, or a different guide style. The rod is almost right for you, but not quite. So you shop around a little more, look at other models and brands, and finally settle on one that's fairly close to your ideal. But it isn't perfect.

Of course. the fish don't care if the rod isn't perfect, but still it nags at you in the back of your mind. It would be a great rod, if only....

But it doesn't have to be that way, you know. You can have *exactly* the fly rod you want. In most things perfection is rarely obtainable, but that's certainly not the case with fly rods. Obtaining your ideal rod is almost as simple as deciding upon its specifications and then having it custom built for you.

Sounds expensive, you say? Not at all! In fact, you can obtain your custom built fly rod for as much as fifty percent less than a mass produced ready-made model. With luck, the savings might be even greater. So what's the catch? There isn't any, really. All you have to do is assemble the rod yourself.

Unfortunately, as soon as some anglers hear the words "do-it-yourself," they throw up their hands and say, "There's no way I could do it! I'm all thumbs." Or, "I tried tying flies once, and just couldn't get the hang of it. I'm sure that I couldn't build a fly rod." Another favorite is, "I'm no good at that sort of thing. Besides, I don't have either the time or all of the tools and equipment that I'd need."

And to all of these excuses my reply is the same, "Not true. If you want to do it, you can." The fact is that assembling a fly rod from component parts requires no special talent or equipment, and very little time. The project is well within the abilities of any fly fisherman, and the rewards are many.

For me it's a toss-up which is the greater reward. My first rods were built years ago when I was a student and simply could not afford to buy a ready-made rod of the quality I desired. It was pure economics to assemble my own. As I recall, the very first rod I made cost under fifteen dollars.

I discovered a ready-made rod for about $6.95 in a discount store. The rod felt good to me, but the fittings and workmanship were definitely second class. But I could afford the $6.95 so I bought the rod, stripped it down to the bare blank, and reassembled it with fittings of my own choosing. When it was finished, you'd better believe I was proud of it. I had a custom built rod that was exactly what I wanted, its cost was well within my budget, and I had the extreme satisfaction of knowing that I'd done it myself.

From then on, I have been hooked as a rod builder, and today I'd do it even if it were more expensive. The personal satisfaction and the ability to have exactly the rod I want are reward enough. The fact that I'm also saving a considerable amount of money is a bonus. I've also discovered that an additional advantage of knowing how to build rods is that now I also know how to repair them. A loose guide, poorly fitting ferrule, damaged cork, or a broken reel seat no longer present serious problems.

Incidentally, that first fly rod was built almost twenty-five years ago. I still have it, and I always feel a touch of pride when I slip it from its well worn case.

There are basically two ways to approach your first rod. You can buy a complete kit of materials, or you can select each component separately from various suppliers. In the latter case, you are, in effect, assembling your own kit.

Either method has certain advantages, but unless the complete kit contains exactly the hardware you want, it is usually best to select the components individually. After all, a big reason for doing the job yourself is to produce your "ideal" rod. Then too, the pouring over catalogs to plan the rod and choose the components is almost half of the fun.

In the not too distant past, finding components from which to build a high quality fly rod was rather difficult. Fortunately, that's no longer the case, and today's rod craftsman never had it so good. Almost every fly fishing specialty shop carries a few rod blanks and other hardware, and most large mail order houses include a wide range of materials in their catalogs. In addition, several suppliers cater exclusively to the home rod builder.

Once the decision has been made to create your own rod, the first consideration is the selection of the blank itself. Will it be of split bamboo, glass, boron or graphite? How long will it be? What weight line will it carry? The answers to these questions, of course, will depend upon your individual needs, but you can be sure that whatever your choice, a suitable blank is available.

For the beginner, it is sometimes difficult to decide which of the many blanks available will be exactly the right one. It may be hard to tell from a catalog description just how the finished rod will feel in your hand. This problem can be solved in several ways.

Since many major rod companies now sell blanks that are identical to their completed rods, one of the best ways to select a blank is to find a factory rod that has the action you desire and then order the matching blank.

If you can visit a shop that stocks a fairly complete line of blanks, you can, of course, sort through them until you find one that feels right. You should remember, though, that the bare blank will feel considerably stiffer than the complete rod, since the addition of the guides and wraps will slow down the action. This is especially true in the case of graphite and boron blanks, which require casting with the proper line to bring out the action.

One technique that may be helpful in evaluating the action of a blank is to place its tip on the floor and hold the butt about head high. Look at the natural bend in the blank. Then apply various amounts of downward hand pressure to the butt and observe the flex pattern. This should allow you to determine whether or not the blank has basically a tip action (fast), medium action, or (slow) butt action with a full flex into the grip area.

A third method for selecting a blank, and the method that many anglers will be forced to use, is to make your selection from a catalog description alone. While this would appear to be the most risky way to obtain exactly the action you want, it really isn't. Undoubtedly, you will be able to narrow your choice down to two or three blanks listed in the catalog. When ordering, you should write a good description of exactly what you want and let the supplier use his judgement in making the final decision from these alternatives. And *always* ask the supplier for permission to exchange the blank if the one sent does not meet your specifications. If such permission will not be granted, have him refund your money and not ship the blank. You will find that most suppliers will go out of their way to see that you are completely satisfied.

In addition to the blank itself, a major consideration will be the reel seat. A wide range of seats is available to suit any taste including up-locking, down-locking, cork inserts, wood inserts, double locking rings, sliding rings, full metal, and those with extension butts. In most cases, the craftsman will bore out the reel seat to fit the butt of the rod, but if a full metal seat is ordered, be sure to also order wood or cork filler so the seat can be matched to the rod.

Cork grips can be purchased pre-shaped in a variety of styles, or the rod crafter can buy either loose cork rings or rings that have been pre-glued into a straight stick so they can be sanded to any shape desired. The standard fly rod grip is six inches in length, which requires twelve half-inch-thick rings. If a sliding ring, cork reel seat is to be built, an additional eight rings are required. Of course, grips of other dimensions will require the appropriate number of rings. If there is any question as to the proper inner diameter of the rings needed to fit your particular rod, ask your supplier to send them in the proper size.

The majority of glass, boron and graphite blanks will be sent with an integral ferrule, and most bamboo blanks will have the ferrule mounted. Be sure to check the catalog description, though, to be certain that such is the case. If you plan to order a one piece blank and cut it to your own dimensions — say for a staggered ferrule — be sure to indicate the point at which you plan to cut it, and ask the supplier to measure it at that point and supply the proper ferrule.

A set of guides, including a stripping guide, hook keeper, and tip top, and size A thread in your preferred color are all the parts needed to complete. If you want to add narrow trim wraps to the guide windings, be sure to order a second color of thread in the same size. Some rod builders like to add a "winding check" to the front edge of the cork grip as a nice finishing touch. This should be ordered with the other components, and you should ask your supplier to send a winding check in a size that is appropriate for the specific blank ordered.

In addition to the above hardware, you will need a small bottle of color preserver, a small bottle of spar varnish, epoxy or other finish for the thread wraps, and some epoxy glue for securing the cork grip and reel seat to the blank. Weldwood plastic-resin glue will also do an excellent job on the grip and reel seat and should be the glue of choice if you plan to glue your own rings together to form the grip. You might also want to order a cloth rod bag and metal rod case in a size to fit your rod.

An assortment of sandpaper, a roll of masking tape, a razor blade, a quarter-inch camel hair brush, a pencil or crayon, a small sharpening stone or fine toothed file and a round "rat tail" file are all of the tools needed to complete the project. An electric hand drill can be helpful in shaping the cork grip, but is not an absolute necessity. If you would like to inscribe your name or other information on the butt of the rod, a fine pointed dip pen, a small bottle of India draftsman's ink and some fine steel wool will be needed. (If you have a dark graphite blank, be certain to get white or a light-colored ink.)

Prior to beginning the assembly of your rod, it is necessary to locate the "spine" of the rod blank. Regardless of the material from which it is made — bamboo, glass, boron, or graphite — slight variations in the manufacturing process will cause one side of the blank to be somewhat more stiff than the other sides. This stiff side is called the "spine," and it will be a reference point for the placement of the guides and reel seat.

There is some disagreement among rod builders concerning exactly where to locate guides relative to a rod's spine. For my thoughts on the matter, refer to Chapter 24.

Before attempting to locate the rod's spine, wrap each end of both rod sections with one turn of masking tape; then when you have determined the "guide side" of the blank, mark it with a pencil on each of the pieces of tape. These lines will serve as reference points during the assembly of the rod. Also a word of warning. *Do not bend the joined rod sections with a great deal of force to "feel the action" until thread wraps have been placed around the open end of the female ferrule.* If too much force is applied, the unwrapped ferrule may split.

After locating the "guide side" of the blank, the first step in the assembly of the rod will depend upon the type of reel seat selected. If the rod is to have a skeleton type cork reel seat with either sliding or locking rings, it must be glued to the rod first. Some rod craftsmen glue the reel seat to the blank as the first step regardless of the type of seat used, and that method will produce satisfactory results. However, I prefer to mount all other types of seat at a later stage in the rod construction.

For the sake of simplicity, we'll assume that you are not using the skeleton type seat, but one of metal or metal-wood construction. If you are using the skeleton type, the instructions for forming and shaping the cork grip will also apply to the reel seat. Just remember to make the reel seat before the grip.

There are three options for making the cork grip. A pre-shaped grip can be purchased and merely glued to the blank, individual cork rings can be glued in place on the blank and later shaped into a grip, or you can glue the rings together before securing them to the rod and shaping them. The first method, of course, is the easiest, but either of the other two techniques permit greater flexibility in the grip design for a truly custom fit. I generally prefer the second method and proceed as follows.

Measure the length of your reel seat, and mark off this distance on the butt of the rod. This mark will indicate where the first cork ring of the grip is to be glued.

Twelve half-inch-thick cork rings will be required to form the standard six-inch grip, but an appropriate number can be used to form the grip length of your choice. The inner diameter of the rings should permit them to slide easily to within a foot or so of their final position, but they should fit quite tightly when slid into place. Ream the hole in the rings to the appropriate size with either a rattail file or a drill bit being very careful to maintain a uniform diameter and not chip the edges of the cork. If possible, do a minimum amount of filing on the ring that will form the front edge of the grip so it will conform tightly to the blank. When reaming the rings, it is best to have them a little snug, since the glue will lubricate them and help them slide into place.

Before gluing the rings into place, lightly sand the area of the blank which they will cover to provide a better gluing surface.

I prefer Weldwood Plastic Resin glue for cork work. Dab a little glue on the blank just ahead of the index mark for the bottom of the reel seat and force the first ring into position. Next, cover the front surface of the first ring and a short section of the blank with glue, and force the second ring into place. Proceed in this manner until all of the rings are in position. During the positioning of the rings, take care to apply sufficient pressure to force adjacent rings together and eliminate all open spaces between them. Keep a damp cloth handy to wipe away the excess glue as it is squeezed from between the rings. When all of the rings are in place and a final check for open spaces has been made, set the rod aside in a warm place and allow the glue to dry for twenty-four hours. If you plan to get into the hobby of building rods, you might want to purchase special clamps that are available to hold the rings tightly in place while the glue is drying.

If you prefer to glue the rings together prior to cementing them to the blank, a piece of threaded steel rod can be used as a mandrel. After the rings have been reamed to fit the blank as described above, screw a nut and large washer onto one end of the threaded rod. Apply glue to the face of each ring and slip them into place over the mandrel. When all of the rings are in place, screw another washer and nut onto the front end of the threaded rod and apply enough pressure to force the rings tightly together. This method of pressure gluing will insure that all spaces between the rings have been eliminated.

After twenty-four hours, remove the rough grip from the mandrel and glue it to the rod blank making sure that it is positioned on the mark which indicates the forward end of the reel seat.

After inspecting many home-crafted rods, I have come to the conclusion that the shaping of the grip is one of the two most critical steps in producing a high quality finished product. Unfortunately, many otherwise excellent rods are ruined by a poorly shaped grip. Most amateur rod builders lack a rod lathe and attempt to shape the grip by hand with generally poor results. Such grips are usually oversized and clumsy, and have a very "clubby" feeling in the finished rod. While the final shape or grip style is up to the builder, it should fit comfortably in the hand, require little effort to hold, and create the impression that the rod is merely an extension of the arm and wrist.

It is quite easy to produce such a grip, and the results are well worth the small amount of extra effort. The secret to success lies in rigging a "lathe" from an electric drill. As shown in the illustrations, jigs can be constructed from scrap wood to hold the drill in a horizontal position and to support the rod. Wrap masking tape around the end of the rod sections before securing them in the drill chuck, and only tighten the chuck to the point where the rod will not slip. *Do not overtighten.*

Position the rod supports just in front of and just behind the rough cork grip, and wrap masking tape around the rod where it will make contact with the supports. Before attempting to shape the grip, turn on the drill and check to be sure that the supports are properly positioned to prevent the rod from wobbling. You will probably find that a slight downward pressure is required to hold the blank onto the supports. This pressure can be provided by the hands during the shaping process.

Before beginning to turn down the grip, it is a good idea to slip the reel seat onto the blank and trace its outer diameter onto the back cork ring. The reel seat should be removed during the turning process.

While the drill is turning the rod, rough shape the grip with course sandpaper (80 grit is about right). Leave the cork slightly oversize as the final smoothing process will take it down to its correct final dimensions. Be careful, too, not to turn down the rear of the grip to a smaller

A handy rod lathe for turning down the cork grip can be assembled from scrap wood and an electric drill.

Commercial rod rests are also available for use with rod lathes, and are a good investment for those who build rods for a hobby.

A rod support for use with the electric drill "lathe" can be constructed from scrap wood.

A rod support for use with the electric drill "lathe" can be constructed with two ball bearing casters and scrap wood.

diameter than that of the reel seat. Use the previously drawn line on the cork as a guide.

The final shaping, smoothing, and polishing of the grip is done with a series of successively finer grades of sandpaper, ending with a 400 or 600 grit wet or dry paper used dry to produce a satin smooth finish.

If a metal reel seat with a hardwood insert is used, all that is required is to bore or ream out the wood insert to fit the butt of the rod and glue it into place with epoxy. If the reel seat has a loose butt cap, this should also be glued into place with epoxy after the seat has been attached to the rod.

When using a full metal reel seat, it will first be necessary to build up the butt of the rod to fit the inside diameter of the seat. This is often done by simply wrapping the rod with many layers of masking tape, but I much prefer to buy or make a wood or cork "filler plug" to fit between the rod and the reel seat. Many reel seats can be purchased complete with a plug. However, if yours did not come that way, one can easily be made from cork rings threaded on a steel mandrel or directly on the blank as described for the grip. If the filler plug is to be made directly on the blank, this should be done before gluing on the rings for the grip.

When gluing the reel seat to the blank, *be sure to align the reel position with the side of the blank upon which the guides will be placed.*

After the reel seat is completed, mount the tip top to the end of the tip section of the blank with five-minute epoxy. *Be sure to align the tip top with the index mark on the tape that indicates the position of the guides.* Before gluing, the tip top should fit smoothly over the blank without either excessive tightness or looseness, and the blank's surface should be roughened slightly with sandpaper to provide a better bond with the epoxy.

Inspection of the snake guides will show that the edge of each foot is rather square. To produce a first class job of wrapping, these square edges must be smoothly tapered with a fine toothed file or a small hook sharpening stone. Be very careful when tapering the feet not to produce a sharp edge anywhere on the guide. Such an edge will cut the wrapping thread, or worse, will score the blank itself during the constant flexing while casting and fishing, leading ultimately to severe rod damage or breakage. After tapering the foot, I usually make one light pass over its bottom edge with a sharpening stone to slightly round it off.

A wide variety of commercial thread tensioning devices are available, and if you plan to make rod building a hobby, such a tool would be a wise investment. On the other hand, a very functional tension method using a drinking glass and a heavy book will produce fine results for the occasional craftsman.

Measure and mark the guide locations on the blank according to the specifications included with your kit or those shown at the end of this chapter. A soft pencil, wax crayon, or thin strips of masking tape can be used to mark the blank.

For convenience, sort the guides and lay them aside in decreasing order of size. Fasten the large stripping guide into position with a strip of masking tape over one foot *being careful to align the guide with the index mark indicating the side of the rod upon which the guides are to be placed.* The index marks, the guide, and the reel position should all be in alignment.

In preparation for wrapping the guides, cut approximately ten inches of thread and set it aside for later use.

With the wrapping thread in the tension device, make one turn of thread around the blank approximately an eighth-inch in front of the loose guide foot. Cross the "tensioned thread" over the free end and rotate the rod to wrap over the free end of the thread securing it to the rod (see illustration). After the thread is securely fastened to the rod, the remainder of the exposed free end can be cut off close to the wraps.

Continue rotating the rod and wrapping the thread up over the foot of the guide until approximately one half of the foot has been covered by thread. Take care to wrap the thread evenly with no spaces between adjacent turns, and use your thumbnail to push the wraps together if spaces should develop. This is very important, as even the most minute spaces will show up as gaping holes when the wraps have been finished. To avoid a gap in the thread where it passes over the end of the guide foot, it is important that all wraps are made *from the blank toward the guide* rather than in the reverse direction.

When about half of the guide foot has been wrapped, pick up the ten-inch piece of thread which was previously cut, double it over to form a loop, and lay the loop onto the blank over the just completed wraps with the closed end of the loop pointing toward the guide (see illustration). Continue wrapping the thread over the rod, the guide foot, and the loop until the entire foot has been covered.

While maintaining tension on the wrapping thread, cut it free from the tensioning device leaving a tag end four to six inches long. Tuck this tag end of thread through the loop that was placed under the wraps, and pull the free ends of the loop, drawing the tag end of thread up tight and locking it against the completed wraps (see illustration). *Do NOT pull the tag end of the thread completely through and under the completed wraps.* Instead, cut off the tag end as close as possible to the completed wraps, and give the loop a quick tug. This will tuck the free end of thread back under the completed wraps and remove the loop from under them.

If the tag end of thread is pulled completely through the wraps before being cut off — as in the manner usually described — it is almost impossible to avoid leaving a short stub of thread protruding from the wrap. This stub will collect finish when the finish is applied and an unsightly bump will result.

Remove the masking tape from the other foot of the guide and wrap it in a similar manner. When the guide is completely wrapped, check its alignment with the index mark. If there is a slight misalignment, the guide can be shifted lightly in either direction by finger pressure.

Wrap the remaining guides into position, constantly checking their alignment. A very convenient way to check guide alignment is to lay the rod section on a flat surface and roll it over until the edges of the guides just touch the surface. All of the guides should touch at the same time, and any that are out of line will be immediately obvious.

When all of the guides have been wrapped, short sections of thread wrapping should be placed over the forward edge of the female ferrule and over the last half-inch of the Male ferrule to strengthen it if it is of the glass-to-glass or graphite-to-graphite style. To provide maximum strength, I like to make the latter wrap a double layer of thread.

Short trim wraps should also be placed next to the tip top, in front of the grip or winding check, and anywhere else desired. Short trim sections of a contrasting color can also be applied at the ends of the guide at this point. If a hook keeper is used, it is generally wrapped into place along with the winding check or grip trim.

I usually wrap a short (one-eighth inch) trim section twenty inches up from the butt of the rod to serve as a measuring point for estimating the length of fish. Such a wrap can be placed at any convenient point and is very handy.

As mentioned earlier, shaping the grip was one of the two most important steps in producing a high quality appearance in the finished rod. The other important factor is the care taken in winding and finishing the thread wraps. A poor wrapping job can completely destroy the rod's appearance.

Any competent woodworker knows that a good finish begins with the preparation of the wood's surface, and the same is true when finishing rod wraps. When all of the guides and trim wraps have been completed, give the guides one final inspection for alignment, and inspect the wraps to be sure there are no spaces between any of the turns of thread.

Normal handling during the wrapping process will tend to fray the thread slightly, and this fuzz should be removed by singeing with a flame before applying a finish to the wraps. An alcohol lamp is ideal for this singeing process, but with care, a candle will do the job nicely.

To singe the wraps, hold them close *beside* the flame and rotate the rod smoothly and quickly. Do not hold the rod *over* the flame or rotate it too slowly or you will burn the thread and have to rewrap the guide.

The use of color preserver on the thread wraps is a point of some disagreement among rod builders. Color preserver is a quick-drying liquid that is applied to the wraps to prevent them from changing color when they are finished. Unfortunately, this color change is prevented by not allowing the finish to soak into the thread. But, if the finish doesn't soak through, the thread is not bonded as tightly to the rod. On the other hand, the use of color preserver does often improve the rod's appearance. My own opinion? Sometimes I use it and sometimes I don't depending upon the situation. When I do use it, I have found that the very best is called "Brilliance" which is sold by Dale Clemens. Unlike most other color preservers, Brilliance produces a very strong and durable wrap when applied as directed.

The classic finish used on the wraps is marine spar varnish. I often

Begin the wrap by winding the thread over itself for several turns, and cutting off the excess. Start the wrap approximately 1/16" to 1/8" from the foot of the guide and wrap toward the guide. Wrapping in this direction will prevent a gap in the turns of thread from forming when the thread is wound onto the guide.

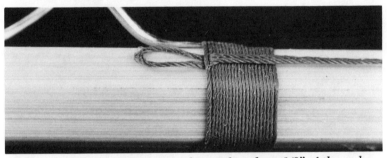

When the guide has been wrapped to within about 1/8" of the end, form a small loop from a short piece of thread, and bind it under the thread wraps. Note: The closed end of the loop must point in the direction you are wrapping.

When the guide has been completely wrapped, cut the winding thread and place its end through the loop which has been bound under the wraps. Pull on the free ends of the loop until the binding thread just begins to pulled under the wraps. Cut off the end of the thread as close as possible to the wraps and give a quick tug to the free ends of the loop. The end of the binding thread will be pulled under itself, and the loop will slip free. DO NOT attempt to pull the binding thread completely back through the wraps before cutting it off. If done in this manner, it will be impossible to prevent leaving a short "stub" of thread protruding from the wraps, and the stub will collect varnish to form an unsightly lump. The end of the binding thread must be cut off close to the wrap when it is at the stage illustrated.

*The electric rotisserie unit from a charcoal grill makes an excellent
devise for rotating a rod while the varnish on the wraps dries. Use it
with any of the rod rests shown in other photos.*

use it on cane rods and it is an excellent choice for all rods. There are,
however, a number of epoxy-type finishes available under several trade
names, and these produce a nice finish on glass, boron and graphite
blanks. My favorite is Crystal Coat, also available from Dale Clemens.

Regardless of the type of finish used, the secret lies in using a sufficient number of coats to produce a smooth, glass-like surface on the
wraps. With the exception of a couple of brands of epoxy, one or two
coats will not produce the desired results. Plan to use four or more coats
until the wraps dry with a high gloss.

Most rod builders apply the finish to the wraps with a soft, narrow
camel hair brush, and this can do a fine job. However, unless care is
used, a brush can cause air bubbles to develop in the finish, and I
generally do not use one. Instead, I use a trick shown to me by one of
my students a few years ago — apply the finish with a needle.

A fly tyer's dubbing needle is perfect, but even a hat pin stuck
through a small cork will work. Merely dip the needle into the finish
and spread it onto the thread wraps. Place only a small amount of
finish on the needle at one time — a single drop will usually be sufficient. Incidentally, if you are using spar varnish, it flows better if kept

warm. Heat it in a pan of water before use, and then let the bottle stand in warm water while you are using it.

Apply the finish in thin coats to prevent runs and drips while drying. For a really first class job, commercial rod builders rotate the rod section while the finish is drying which completely eliminates unsightly drips. Such a "rod rotator" can easily be rigged by the home rod builder, and the results really do justify the small effort involved.

My device uses the electric unit from the rotisserie of our charcoal grill and a couple of rod rests. Place a wooden dowel into the electric unit where the spit normally fits, and attach the rod section to the dowel with a short length of rubber tubing. Stand the motor on end, lay the rod (with freshly finished wraps) across the rod rests, and turn on the motor. The rod should be allowed to rotate until the finish has time to set.

After the wraps have been finished to your satisfaction, a final touch can be added to the rod by inscribing it with your name, its length, weight and line size. This is easily done with draftsman's (India) ink. Decide where you want the inscription placed and lightly buff the area with very fine steel wool to remove the gloss from the blank. Use an old-fashioned dip pen and ink of a contrasting color on the blank to inscribe the desired information. When the ink is dry, use your fingertip to spread a drop or two of the finish used for the wraps in a layer over the inscription. Add a second coat when the first is dry.

And there you have it! Your "ideal rod" is finished and you did it yourself. You have a right to be proud.

GUIDE SPACING CHARTS
Courtesy of The Orvis Co.
Suggested Measurements for Guide Spacing

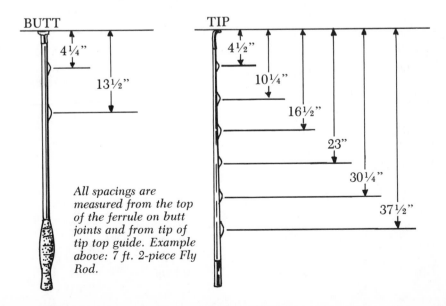

BUTT

TIP

4¼"

13½"

4½"

10¼"

16½"

23"

30¼"

37½"

All spacings are measured from the top of the ferrule on butt joints and from tip of tip top guide. Example above: 7 ft. 2-piece Fly Rod.

FLY RODS
Graphite
5 ft.1 pc.
From tip end
5¼"
11¼"
19"
27"
35"

FLY RODS
Graphite
6½ ft.3 pc.
Butt
3"
Middle
2½"
7½"
13¾"
20¼"
Tip
4¾"
10¼"
16¼"
23"

FLY RODS
Graphite
7½ ft.2 pc.
Butt
5"
16½"
Tip
4-3/8"
9¾"
15-5/8"
21-5/8"
28"
34-7/8"
42½"

FLY RODS
Graphite
6½ ft.2 pc.
Butt
2-5/8"
13"
Tip
4½"
11"
18¼"
26"
34-5/8"

FLY RODS
Graphite
7ft.2 pc.
Butt
4¼"
13½"
Tip
4½"
10¼"
16½"
23"
30¼"
37½"

FLY RODS
Graphite
7 ft.9 in.2 pc.
Butt
5"
16½"
Tip
5-1/8"
10½"
16"
22"
28¼"
35"
44"

FLY RODS
Graphite
7 ft.11 in.
Butt
7-7/8"
19¼"
Tip
5-1/8"
10½"
16"
22"
28¼"
35½"
44"

FLY RODS
Graphite
8 ft.3 in.2 pc.
Butt
7-7/8"
19¼"
Tip
4-7/8"
10-7/8"
17-5/8"
24½"
31½"
38¾"
46-5/8"

FLY RODS
Graphite
9 ft.2 pc.
Butt
4"
12-5/8"
23½"
Tip
5"
10½"
16¼"
22-3/8"
28½"
35"
41¾"
49"

FLY RODS
Graphite
8 ft.2 pc.
Butt
7-7/8"
19¼"
Tip
5-1/8"
10½"
16"
22"
28¼"
35½"
44"

FLY RODS
Graphite
8½ ft.2 pc.
Butt
3-7/8"
12-1/8"
21½"
Tip
4-7/8"
10-7/8"
17-5/8"
24½"
31½"
38¾"
46-5/8"

FLY RODS
Graphite
9 ft.3 in.2 pc.
Butt
4"
12½"
23½"
Tip
5"
10¼"
16¼"
22½"
29"
35¾"
43"
51"

FLY RODS
Graphite
  8 ft.3 pc.
Butt
  3½"
Middle
  2-7/8"
  9¾"
  18-3/8"
  27-1/8"
Tip
  4-5/8"
  9¾"
  5-3/8"
  21½"
  27-5/8"

FLY RODS
Graphite
  8 ft.9 in.2 pc.
Butt
  3-7/8"
  12-1/8"
  21½"
Tip
  5"
  10½"
  16¼"
  22-3/8"
  28½"
  35"
  41¾"
  49"

FLY RODS
Graphite
  9½ ft.2 pc.
Butt
  4"
  12½"
  22½"
Tip
  5"
  10-3/8"
  16-3/8"
  22½"
  29"
  35¾"
  43"
  51"

FLY RODS
Graphite
  10 ft.2 pc.
Butt
  6"
  14½"
  24¼"
Tip
  4½"
  9-3/8"
  14½"
  19¾'
  26¾"
  33½"
  40½"
  48"
  55½"

FLY RODS
Graphite
  11 ft.3 pc.
Butt
  5½"
  14-5/8"
Middle
  4½"
  12½"
  20½"
  29"
  37½"
Tip
  6¼"
  12-1/8"
  8-3/8"
  23¾"
  31-7/8"
  39"

FLY RODS
Graphite
  10 ft.3 pc.
Butt
  7¼"
Middle
  3¼"
  10½"
  18¼"
  26¼"
  34¾"
Tip
  5"
  10½"
  16"
  22¼"
  28¾"
  35¼"

FLY RODS
Graphite
  10½ ft.3 pc.
Butt
  5½"
  15¼"
Middle
  5¼"
  11¾"
  19¾"
  27¼"
  36¼"
Tip
  5¼"
  10¾"
  16¾"
  23½"
  30¼"
  37"

FLY RODS
Graphite
  13½ ft.3 pc.
Butt
  11"
Middle
  4½"
  14¼"
  24¾"
  35¾"
  47¾"
Tip
  6½"
  13"
  20¼"
  29"
  38"
  47¾"

24.

Thoughts on Fly Rod Guide Position

Almost anyone who has ever assembled a fly rod from a blank has read and rigorously followed instructions for locating the rod's spine in order to wrap the guides along its stiffest side. Such a procedure has been standard for many years and was developed to place the guides in a position to best utilize the rod's "backbone" while casting and playing fish.

Without giving the matter a great deal of thought, I have slavishly followed this practice myself when building rods and have even written a number of articles instructing others how to do it. Several years ago, however, I came to the considered opinion that this traditional method of positioning fly rod guides is *absolutely wrong*.

It's difficult to make a statement that flies in the face of tradition and the opinions of many great rod makers, and it may generate howls of protest. However, I'll stand by my statement, and, if nothing else, it may stimulate some thought and other comments on the matter.

Before you jump up to write an angry letter to the editor, however, consider how we are instructed to locate a rod's spine or stiff side. We are told to apply a bending pressure to the rod section, and then roll it until we locate the side that seems to "kick over." The place where the rod "kicks over" is the stiff side, and we are told to locate the guides either along this side (the major spine) or on the side directly opposite to it (the minor spine).

But think about what we have been asked to do. We have been told to place the guides along the side of the rod that places the rod in an *unstable position*. That is, the rod does not want to be bent in that direction or to stay in that position—it wants to "kick over" and assume a more stable position.

Have you ever noticed that while fishing your rod often twists so the reel is pointing off in some direction to the side of that in which you're casting? It happens because we are not able to cast with the spine of the rod always precisely in the plane of the cast, and the rod, being in a basically unstable position, "kicks over."

The solution to the problem is simple. The guides should be placed along the side of the rod that is at right angles to the spine. To locate this position, proceed as if you were trying to find the spine, but allow the rod to "kick over" and assume its stable position. Mark this side of the rod. When you repeat the procedure, i.e., bend the rod and roll it, you will find that the rod always wants to come to rest with the mark on the concave side of the bend. That is where to place the guides.

In addition to preventing rod twist and producing a rod that casts very smoothly, positioning the guides in this manner places the major and minor spines along the sides of the rod while casting. The added lateral stiffness then helps to dampen unwanted sideways vibration of the rod tip, and produces a more accurate cast.

The traditional reason for placing the guides along the rod's spine was to utilize the extra stiffness while casting and playing fish. However, with today's modern rod materials and adhesives, I don't believe that the very slight gain in stiffness outweighs the inherent disadvantages of the method. In fact, it is unlikely that most anglers can tell the difference in the small amount of stiffness that is gained by the traditional method of guide placement with modern graphite and boron rods.

It always pleases me when someone, after trying one of my handmade split bamboo rods, comments on how smooth and stable it seems to be. Now my secret is out—I'm convinced that such performance is the result of my placement of the guides. And I'm convinced that you will notice a considerable improvement in your rod's performance with this method. It will cast more smoothly, be more stable, and will not twist while casting.

You may find it hard to believe, but give the method a try before you condemn it.

25.

New Life for Old Bamboo

I wish I had a dollar for every bent old bamboo fly rod that lies forgotten and gathering dust in dark corners of hundreds of attics across the country. I'd even be happy with a dollar for every time someone has come to me with "Grandpa's old rod" to see if it could be reconditioned "just for old time's sake."

Though warped, scratched, missing a few guides, and possibly with a broken tip, most of these rods can quite easily be put back into nearly original condition. It may not pay to have the job done by a professional, but almost any fisherman is capable of doing the work himself in a few hours.

Before beginning a do-it-yourself refinishing job on an old rod, though, you should first attempt to determine whether or not the rod is a valuable old classic built by one of the well known early rod makers. If such is the case, the rod should be reconditioned by an expert or its value can be greatly decreased. If the label or inscription on the rod cannot be read, one tip-off that it may be a high quality rod will be whether or not it is in a metal rod tube. This, of course, is not infallible, but is one clue.

You can also ask yourself whether or not the original owner of the rod would likely have been the type of person to have had a first-class classic rod. If there is any doubt in your mind regarding the possible value of the rod, it should be evaluated by an expert before you decide whether or not to refinish it yourself.

If you decide to do the job yourself, the first step is to examine the rod to determine what work is required and which parts need replacing.

Begin by flexing each rod section along each of its sides to see if the bamboo is split or separated. Then, join the sections to check the fit of the ferrules. A "clicking" sound or a feeling of "looseness" when the rod is swung back and forth in a casting arc indicates either that the ferrule itself is worn out, or that the glue has dried out and the ferrule is no longer fastened tightly to the cane. Close inspection of the ferrule will reveal which of these is the cause of the problem. If the parts are worn, they should be replaced, but, if the glue has merely dried out, the original ferrule can be refitted.

A visual check of the cork grip and reel seat will show their condition, and a quick sighting down the length of the rod will indicate whether there are any sets that will require straightening.

As a routine practice, all of the old line guides should be replaced, since worn guides can quickly ruin an expensive fly line.

The last step in the preliminary check is to inspect the rod finish for cracks, chips, and peeling, and decide whether a complete refinishing job is called for, or if a slight touch up will do the trick.

Stripping Down the Rod

Prior to removing the guides, measure and record their locations so the new ones can be accurately placed, then remove them by carefully cutting their thread windings with a razor blade. The tip top is removed by very carefully rotating it over a source of heat, which will soften the glue and allow the top to be pulled off. Care must be taken to avoid excessive heat which will char and weaken the bamboo.

If the ferrules and reel seat are to be removed, they can be heated and pulled free as was done with the tip top. Again, excessive heat must be avoided. The ferrules of many early rods were secured with fine wire pins in addition to cement, and, if such pins are found on your rod, they must be carefully driven out with a small punch.

The cork grip and reel seat plug can simply be cut away with a sharp hunting knife.

If the rod is to be completely refinished, the old varnish must be scraped off with a single edged razor blade, the edge of a piece of broken glass, or a similar tool. Avoid the temptation to use a chemical paint remover as this may dissolve the glue that holds the rod together. Extreme care must be taken while scraping, since the bamboo's power fibers lie just below the surface, and they must not be removed or damaged. When the rod has been completely scraped, it should be *lightly* sanded with 220 grade sandpaper followed by 400 or 600 grade wet or dry paper.

Repairing Broken Sections

A bamboo rod may be broken in several different ways. It may be broken off flush with the ferrule, the tip may be broken off near the end, or a section may be split without being broken completely off. Most of these problems can be repaired to produce a usable rod.

If the rod is broken off within a few inches of the tip, simply attach a larger tip top at that point. The rod will, of course, be slightly shorter and probably a little more stiff, but should perform reasonably well.

If the break is at the ferrule, the solution is similar. The ferrule is replaced with the loss of only an inch or so of the rod. To remove the broken bamboo from the ferrule, drill a small hole into the stub and turn a small wood screw into the hole. Rotate the ferrule over a heat source to melt the glue, and pull out the stub by grasping the screw with a pliers.

The repair of a split rod section is illustrated in the photographs. Weldwood Plastic Resin glue should be carefully applied to all broken surfaces. Next, bind the broken area with cotton "butcher's string," as illustrated. When repaired, the broken area may not be perfectly straight and will require heat straightening as described below. Do not attempt to straighten this area until reinforcing thread wraps have been made over the break and the section has been revarnished.

To repair a split rod section, separate the split and work a good waterproof glue into all open areas. A fine needle can be used to insure that the glue reaches all parts of the wood.

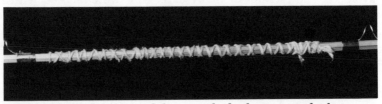

After applying the glue, tightly wrap the broken area in both directions with cotton string, and allow the glue to dry thoroughly.

When repaired, the broken area may not be perfectly straight and will require heat straightening as described below. Do not attempt to straighten this area until reinforcing thread wraps have been made over the break and the section has been revarnished.

The reinforcing wraps are made with white silk or nylon thread at short intervals over the thread using the method described for winding guides. The wraps need be no longer than approximately one-eighth inch each. The varnish or epoxy used to finish the rod will soak into the white thread causing it to almost disappear and the repair will be practically invisible.

Replacing the Ferrule

Before fitting a new ferrule or replacing the old one, the ends of the rod sections should be scraped and sanded to remove all old cement. The new ferrule should fit very snugly, in fact, it is best if it is just a *little* too tight to slip into place by hand.

The method for replacing ferrules is shown in the photographs.

Either a slow drying flexible glue such as Goodyear Pliobond or a fast setting five-minute epoxy can be used for ferrules, but it is best to avoid the stick type ferrule cement which is melted onto the rod. This

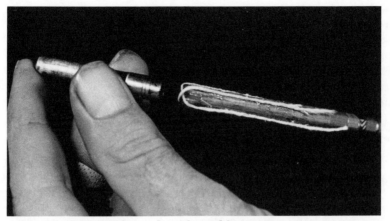

A loosely fitting ferrule can be tightened by crossing cotton string over the end of the rod section and forcing the ferrule into place.

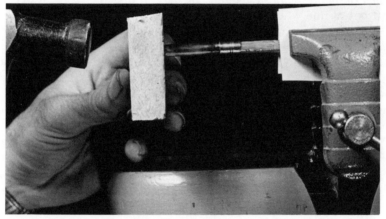

New ferrules should fit the rod section very snugly. Place the rod section into a padded vise, heat the ferrule to expand it slightly, and drive it onto the end of the rod by carefully tapping it with a hammer. The ferrule is protected by a block of wood.

type of cement tends to dry out and loosen with age, so its use is best reserved for temporary field repairs.

Straightening the Rod

With a little careful work, a set or bend in the rod can usually be removed by gently heating the bent area and applying pressure in a direction opposite to the set.

Begin by locating the areas that are out of line and marking them with a penciled "X" on the convex side. The straightening pressure is then applied toward the mark. If several sets are present, they should be straightened one at a time beginning with the most serious one.

Rotate the bent area slowly over a heat source such as an electric or gas stove being very careful not to apply too much heat. The trick is to warm the area evenly and then apply gentle pressure to bend the rod opposite to the set. If the set remains after the rod has cooled, apply a little more heat and a little more pressure until the rod remains straight. As with all rod work, the key is "easy does it." Work carefully and gently, and you'll get the job done.

Replacing the Grip and Reel Seat

If both the cork grip and the reel seat are to be replaced, the reel seat should be done first after both have been removed from the rod.

To install the reel seat, first drill or file the hole in the filler plug to produce a tight fit on the rod butt and glue it in place with waterproof glue or epoxy. When the plug is dry, glue the seat in place *making certain that the reel position will be in line with the side of the rod on which the guides will be wound.* Be careful that the reel seat does not shift out of line when it is set aside to dry.

Either of three methods can be used to replace the cork grip. Pre-shaped grips can be purchased that need only be reamed to fit the rod butt and glued in place; loose cork rings can be glued to the rod and sanded to shape. Or, pre-glued cork rings can be purchased in any length you require and glued in place and shaped. The cork can be glued with a waterproof glue such as Weldwood powdered resin or a five-minute epoxy.

Shaping of the grip is done with a rasp and coarse sandpaper followed by successively finer grades of paper as the desired shape is approached. A final sanding with 400 or 600 grade wet or dry paper will produce a satin smooth finish. (See Chapter 23.)

Finishing the Rod

The final finishing should be done in a dust free area such as the bathroom of your house. The air should be dry, though, so have your family skip their showers the night you plan to do the work.

A variety of finishes can be applied to the rod. Marine spar varnish can be applied in three or four thin coats and is a standard bamboo rod finish. The can of varnish should be warmed in a pan of hot water, which will allow it to flow smoothly onto the rod. The varnish can be applied with a soft brush, but I prefer to use my fingers for the task. Place a large drop of warm varnish on the tip of your finger and simply rub it into the bamboo with long smooth strokes adding more varnish as necessary. When the section is completely covered, make a final wipe of your finger down the entire length of each side to smooth everything out.

The finish I usually prefer is Birchwood-Casey True-Oil gun stock finish applied with my fingers. It dries very quickly, which helps to avoid dust, and it is ready to rub in about three hours. I apply four coats of the True-Oil following each with a light rubbing with very fine rubbing compound and water, which results in a glossy finish. I use a rubbing compound made for model planes, but the automotive type should work as well if it is extra fine. Care must be taken to rub very gently and use plenty of water so as not to remove the finish from the edges of the rod. Be certain that the rod is thoroughly washed and dried following each rubbing so all of the compound is removed. After the final rubbing, a polish with jeweler's rouge will produce a glass-like finish.

Winding the Guides

Some rod builders prefer to wind on the guides before applying the finish to the rod. They then varnish the rod and the windings at the same time. This is a good method, but cannot be used with the True-Oil finish since the substance does not work well with the thread windings. Also, since I like to rub down the finish, I do the rod before the guides are wrapped and finish the wraps separately with varnish or epoxy.

For instructions on wrapping guides please refer to Chapters 23 and 24.

The recondition job is now completed.

With but a few hours of your time, you can add many years of life to a forgotten old rod, which deserves better than to merely gather dust in some dark corner. And, perhaps best of all, you may feel a touch of the pride of workmanship that was experienced by the original craftsmen who created these fine fly rods.

26.

Advanced Casting Techniques

The ability to cast a fly well adds immeasurably to the pleasure of fly fishing, and while the basics of casting are quite simple, there are a few little tricks that can increase an angler's effectiveness on the stream. Thus, the purpose of this chapter is not to teach you *how* to cast, but to share with you a few of the little tricks that have been very useful to me over the years.

The Tailing Loop

The "tailing loop" is a problem that vexes most fly fishers at some time or other. The term refers to the situation where the top leg of the loop in the casting line falls below the bottom leg of the loop during the forward motion of the line. As a result, the fly often snags on the line, or worse, a "wind knot" is tied in the leader. Incidentally, the term "wind knot" is a misnomer. It's nice to be able to blame such knots on the wind, but it ain't so — they really should be called "caster knots," since they are usually caused by a tailing loop or other casting errors, and not the wind.

There are several casting stroke errors that can cause the tailing loop, but in my experience as a casting instructor, I have become convinced that there is one primary cause of the problem for most anglers — that is casting too much with the tip of the rod too soon in the casting stroke. Of course an experienced fly caster can cast with any part of the rod — the tip, mid-section or butt, so it's not casting with the tip alone that causes the tailing loop. It's how you cast with the tip.

Actually, when I'm teaching a class of beginning fly casters, I almost consider it a mark of progress when some of them begin to cast with a tailing loop. Let me explain.

As students become better casters, they attempt to be more crisp in their casting strokes, and they make more of an effort to stop the rod sharply to produce nice loops. That's good. But, unfortunately, in their haste to turn the rod over and stop it, they turn it over too soon. The result is a tip cast with a tailing loop. The same thing often happens to an experienced caster while fishing. He or she makes several very nice false casts, but on the final delivery stroke the rod tip is rushed a bit, tilted forward too soon, and a tailing loop results.

The solution is to "stroke with the whole rod" during the cast, and not just flip the tip. After the rod has stopped on the backcast — say at approximately the one o'clock position, *the rod should remain at that angle and should be pushed forward to start the forward cast. Only after the rod and casting arm have been pushed forward, should the rod tip be turned over and stopped on the forward cast*

An instructional trick that I use when trying to solve this problem for anglers is to suggest that they "lead the cast with the reel." Try to form the mental concept that the reel is pulling the rod forward during the "push," and the reel should move forward in a relatively straight line, not in a vertical arc (See illustration).

Try to accelerate the rod smoothly through the casting stroke, and not just "punch the tip."

The Parallel Loop

A problem that is perhaps even more common than the tailing loop is the inability to cast a parallel loop, that is, a loop in which the top leg is exactly parallel to the bottom leg of the loop during the casting stroke. As a result, the fly swings wildly at the end of the cast, and casting efficiency, distance and accuracy are lost.

A principle that is basic to solving this and many other casting problems is that the line will do what the rod tip does. That is, any movement of the rod tip will be reflected in a similar movement of the fly line. Thus, if we want to cast with a parallel loop, *the rod tip must move forward or backward in a straight line*. If the loop is not parallel, it is because the rod tip has moved in a curved path.

The basic cause of moving the rod tip in a curved path on the forward cast is placing the rod in an improper position at the end of the backcast. The most common cause of placing the rod in the improper position is that the caster rotates the shoulder of the casting arm backward during the backcast. As a result, the rod tip ends up behind the caster's back (see illustration). Then the only way to move the rod forward must be in an arc to get back around the body.

The proper position for the rod tip at the end of the backcast is somewhat to the side of the angler, and the shoulders should remain square to the target. It is then a simple matter to move the rod forward in a straight line during the forward cast (see illustration).

While your rod is stopped at the end of the backcast, try to imagine a vertical line dropped from its tip to the ground. This line should *not* fall behind the body but off to the side of the caster, right side for a right-handed caster, (see illustration).

A little thoughtful practice in the back yard should quickly solve this problem and allow you to produce beautiful parallel loops. When you have mastered it, you will find that you can cast with greater line speed, more distance, and greater accuracy, and you will cast much more effectively in the wind.

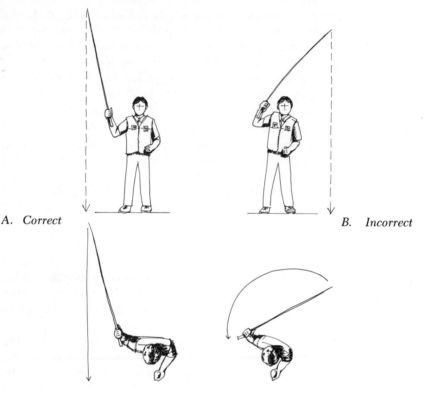

A. *Correct*   B. *Incorrect*

Casting the parallel loop.

A. Correct position. Shoulders square to target, rod tip positioned on angler's casting side. Rod moves forward in a straight line resulting in a parallel loop.

B. Incorrect position. Casting shoulder rotated backward away from target, rod tip positioned behind angler. Rod must move forward in an arc, which will destroy parallel loop.

The Roll Pick-up

Have you ever been fishing bass bugs or panfish poppers and tried to pick up a long line? If so, you know what is likely to happen. As you try to lift the bug from the water, it digs in, dives, and you almost pull your arm out of its socket. If the bug comes up at all, it does so with a loud *pop*, and the line sluggishly falls behind you making a forward cast very difficult, if not impossible.

Or have you ever been fishing with a sinking line or shooting head and tried to pick it up for a backcast? Unless the line is very short, it's all but impossible to do.

Fortunately, there's an easy solution to both of these problems — it's called the roll pick-up.

Most fly fishers are familiar with the roll cast. The roll pick-up is merely an extension of this procedure. To execute the roll pick-up, do a roll cast. When the loop in the line rolls out to the bass bug, the bug will jump straight up out of the water, and, as as soon as it's airborn, simply make a regular backcast. Simple!

The same procedure is used to pick up a sunken line or shooting head. Do a roll cast to bring the line to the surface, and before it has time to sink again, make a regular backcast.

Slack Line, Mid-Air Mends, and Curve Casts

In many fly fishing situations the angler's ability to cast a slack line and leader is of critical importance if the fly is to be prevented from dragging unnaturally on or under the water. But slack alone is not enough. The amount and location of the slack, in addition to the accurate placement of the fly, are important to the success of the cast.

While there are many methods for producing a slack line, there is one technique that I feel is the most effective and versatile. I call it the "wiggle cast."

To produce the wiggle cast, we again make use of the principle that the line will do what the rod tip does. First, make a normal straight cast with a nice tight loop. *After the power stroke has been made and the line is shooting forward*, simply wiggle the rod tip from side to side in a horizontal plane. When done correctly, the fly will land on target, and the line will fall to the water in a series of S-curves. The only trick to the cast is to throw a reasonably tight loop and to wait to put in the wiggles until after the power stroke, when the line is shooting forward. Since the wiggles put slack in the line, you'll have to cast a longer line than usual to reach your target.

With a little experimentation you will find that you have absolute control over the size and number of wiggles that are placed in the line. You can make a few broad sweeps of the rod tip and produce several wide wiggles of slack line, or you can wiggle the rod tip rapidly through many short strokes and produce a series of very small waves in the line.

The wiggle cast is well known and is used by many experienced anglers. However, many fly fishers fail to realize the full potential of the technique. At least as important as its ability to put controlled slack into a cast is its usefulness in mending the line before it falls to the water — the "mid-air mend."

Mending line involves various methods of putting an upstream curve into the line where it crosses a narrow current of fast water on its way to the target (or a downstream loop if it crosses a narrow piece of slow water). Such a loop of slack delays the inevitable drag on the fly that would occur if the line was straight.

As usually practiced, mending is done after the line is on the water during the drift of the fly. Unfortunately, when done in this way, it is often difficult to accurately place the slack where it's needed, especially at long range. And often line-mending itself causes the fly to drag. These problems can be eliminated by mending the line *before* it lands on the water.

To learn the mid-air mend, make a basic wiggle cast, but only put in one wiggle. That is, make a normal cast with a fairly tight loop, and after the power stroke, while the line is shooting forward, quickly move the rod tip either to the right or to the left and then back to its normal position. The result should be a single loop of slack somewhere between the caster and the target. Don't worry, for now, where the loop of slack is placed, but practice making them both to the right and left.

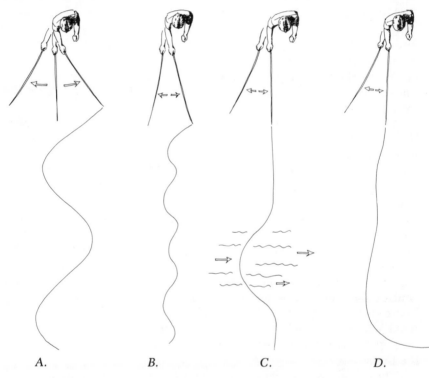

A.   B.   C.   D.

A. Large wiggles produced by moving rod tip parallel to the water in wide sweeps. B. Small wiggles produced by moving rod tip parallel to the water in small sweeps. C. Single mid-air mend produced by a single sweep of the rod tip in the direction of the desired mend. D. Curve cast produced by single sweep of the rod tip in the direction opposite to the desired curve. Rod sweep applied immediately after the stop of the rod on the forward power stroke.

When you can comfortably produce a single loop of slack in either direction, begin working on the accurate placement of the slack line.

To do this you must remember that the placement of the loop depends on *when* it is put into the line. If you want the loop of slack close to you, wait until the line has almost straightened on the forward cast until you put in the wiggle. On the other hand, if you want the loop to be out near the end of the line, put in the wiggle very soon after you make the power stroke of the cast. A little experimentation will show you the proper timing.

To hone your technique, place an obstacle — a rock, jacket, towel or other object — on the ground in front of you and practice casting loops of slack to the right and left around it while the fly lands straight ahead on target. Try it with the obstacle placed at varying distances.

Finally, this same technique can be used to throw a curve cast in which the fly swings around and lands either to the right or left of the line. This is a very effective method when you are casting across a stream toward the bank, and want the fly to drift downstream ahead of the line.

To make such a curve cast, use the same technique as for the mid-air mend, but apply the wiggle *immediately* after the completion of the power stroke of the cast. In fact, the wiggle almost becomes a part of the power stroke — but not quite. You'll still have to stop the rod at the end of the power stroke to form a tight casting loop, but the stop should be extremely brief before wiggling the rod tip to produce a curve in the desired direction. A little practice will give you the idea, and further practice should perfect the technique.

27.

Leader Design
And Construction

M ost novice fly fishers are well aware of the need to consider very thoughtfully the selection of tackle that is appropriate to their specific needs. They take a great deal of time when choosing their first fly rods, lines and reels. Quite likely they will spend many hours pouring over books and catalogs in order to determine exactly which flies are needed.

Unfortunately, one important link in the tackle system is often neglected, and is selected almost as an afterthought with little understanding of its importance to casting and fishing success — *the leader*.

In fly fishing the leader must perform many functions. It must transmit the casting energy from the line to the fly in order to permit the fly to turn over and land properly upon the water. At the same time, it must progressively dissipate the casting energy so the fly will land gently upon the water like the natural insect, rather than plop down with an audible 'splat.' The leader must provide an almost invisible link between the bulky fly line and the delicate fly. And finally, the leader must allow a fly to drift freely on or under the water to give the appearance of a naturally drifting insect. The leader should not create drag on the fly.

A poorly designed leader is an abomination. It will cause the fly to land in a tangled mess of nylon, or cause the fly to land loudly upon the water and frighten wary fish. It will break just as you hook the largest fish of your life, or will be so fat that no fish will approach your fly. It will cause your dry fly or nymph to twist, turn and skate through the water like no insect that has ever lived. Small wonder, then, that experienced anglers expend considerable effort to obtain the correct leaders for their particular fishing situations. The leader can often spell fishing success or failure.

In its most simple form, a leader is merely a level strand of nylon monofilament tied to the end of the fly line. Unfortunately, except possibly for fishing for panfish where the delicacy of the fly presentation is less important, a level leader is a very poor choice. Such a leader will not turn over properly unless it is quite short, and then it will not deliver the fly lightly to the water. A beginner would do well to take a tip from the experts and avoid the level leader.

Just as fly lines are tapered for greater efficiency in casting and delicacy in presentation of the fly, the best leaders are also tapered.

Tapered leaders are available in either of three styles — one piece knotless tapers, braided tapers and compound tapers. The latter are made by joining successively smaller pieces of level monofilament with blood knots until the desired length and taper are obtained. Each style has its own advantages and disadvantages.

Knotless tapered leaders are convenient to use and are particularly good when weeds or debris in the water would tend to collect on the knots of a compound tapered leader. On the other hand, since it is impossible to make your own knotless leaders, they must be purchased, and, thus, may be more expensive than those you can produce yourself.

Secondly, such commercial leaders often are made too light in their butt sections and may not turn over properly. Then too, it may not always be possible to obtain a leader with precisely the desired taper. And, of course, once such a leader has been shortened by a few changes of flies, a new tippet must be tied on, and you then have a knotted leader.

Because of these shortcomings, most experienced fly fishermen generally use compound tapered or braided leaders. Braided leaders are relatively new and are still being improved, but they seem to have great potential. Generally they consist of several feet of a braided butt section with one or more knotted tippet sections. Though they are considerably more expensive than other types of leaders, the braided leaders last much longer, and only the regular monofilament sections are replaced.

Commercially tied compound leaders usually are well designed and function very well, and they are available in a wide variety of lengths and breaking strengths. The real advantage of the compound taper, though, is that it can be easily made at home — or right on the stream — at a fraction of the cost of a ready made leader, and you can build exactly the taper that is needed in a given situation.

While many anglers have their pet leader designs, most of them are based upon the 60/20/20 formula. According to this formula, approximately 60 percent of the leader's length is composed of fairly large diameter material, 20 percent of the length is made up of short pieces which rapidly decrease in diameter, and the final 20 percent is one or two pieces of fine diameter material to make up the light "tippet" which attaches to the fly. Leaders tied to this formula will turn over properly and present the fly fairly well.

When building a leader according to the 60/20/20 formula, it is usual to begin with a butt section that is about two-thirds the diameter of the tip of the fly line. In most cases this will be approximately .019 to .021 inch in diameter. A leader butt of this diameter will bend smoothly with the fly line, and will not cause a collapsing "hinge" effect which will prevent the fly from turning over. The butt section is joined to the fly line with either a nail knot, needle knot or uni-knot.

The successive pieces of material which are joined together should vary from one another by no more than .002 inch in order to maintain knot strength, and to allow the proper transmission of energy. The most widely used knot for joining leader sections is the "blood knot."

In order to avoid having to tie the needle or nail knot when changing leaders on the stream, many anglers leave the butt seciton of the leader permanently attached to the line and make the leader change at the first butt section blood knot, or with a loop-to-loop connection.

The accompanying table lists a variety of leaders that are designed according to the 60/20/20 formula. Any of these tapers will produce an excellent leader, and it is strongly recommended that you follow these patterns for your first attempt at "rolling your own."

It should be noted that in listing the patterns for the leaders in the table, the nylon material is listed according to its *diameter* and *not its breaking strength*. The ability of the leader to transmit the casting energy is based upon its relative diameter, and unfortunately, materials from different manufacturers that have similar breaking strengths probably have different diameters. Thus, if different brands of materials are used in constructing a leader, and they are put together according to only their breaking strengths, nothing will be known about the actual taper of the leader. In such a situation, it is quite likely that the resulting leader will fail to function properly. Therefore, when purchasing leader material, be certain that each spool you buy has both the diameter of the material and its breaking strength shown on the label.

You will also note that the leaders listed are identified both according to their lengths and an "X" number, for example, 3X, 4X, 6X and so on. The "X" designation can be a source of confusion until its meaning is understood. Again, the "X" designation refers to the material's diameter and not its breaking strength.

The "X" designation is really quite simple if you remember the "Rule of 11." According to this rule, leader material identified as "0X" has a diameter of .011 inch. Then, every time you subtract .001 inch from the material's diameter, you add one "X." Thus, material classified as "1X" is .010 inch in diameter, "2X" is .009 inch, "4X" is .007 inch , "7X" is .004 inch and so on. While a few companies produce 8X material, the smallest generally available is the very light 7X (.004 inch).

Several factors determine the proper tippet length and diameter when constructing a compound tapered leader. First, it is important for proper leader performance to match the tippet diameter to the size of the fly with which it will be used. If the tippet is too fine it will lack knot strength when secured to a large fly, and it will not allow a large wind resistant fly to turn over properly. On the other hand, if the tippet is too large in diameter, it will cause unnatural drag on a small fly and may frighten wary fish.

The leader tippet lengths included with the accompanying patterns are very good for general use. However, if particularly air resistant flies are used, and the leader seems to land in a tangled mess rather than neatly turning over, it may be wise to shorten the tippet a few inches at a time until it performs properly. Or, when fishing small flies in very clear water, the tippet may be lengthened. Many expert anglers "fine tune" their tippet lengths with each change of flies.

The accompanying table lists suggested tippet diameters to match various fly sizes. You will note that the categories overlap somewhat. As a general rule, especially with the smaller tippets (5X-7X), it is best to use the listed tippet diameter with fly sizes in the middle of the range shown. However, when necessary, the tippet will work with flies at either end of the range. When fishing for large fish, it may be a good idea to use the heavier of two possible leader tippets, or, when fishing in very clear water, use the smaller of two tippet diameters.

TIPPET VS. HOOK SIZE

Tippet Diameter	Hook Size)	Tippet Diameter	Hook Size
.011 inch(0X)	1/0-4	.006 inch(5X)	14-22
.010 inch(1X)	4-8	.005 inch(6X)	16-24
.009 inch(2X)	6-10	.004 inch(7X)	18-28
.008 inch(3X)	10-14	.003 inch(8X)	18-28
.007 inch(4X)	12-16		

As can be seen from the list of leader patterns, "standard" leaders are often tied either 7½, 9 or 12 feet in length. While there is nothing sacred about these lengths, they do provide an excellent starting point. As you gain experience you may want to vary your leader length considerably to suit the fishing conditions. Personally, I prefer to tie my basic dry fly leader ten feet in length and tapered to 4X at the tippet. Such a configuration permits me to conveniently make needed adjustments as fishing conditions dictate.

For example, should I suddenly come upon a large fish or want to switch to a large fly, I can simply cut the leader back to a heavier section, and I will still have a leader of at least seven feet in length. If I should have to switch to a very small fly or desire a longer leader for very clear water, I can cut back the 4X tippet to about 6 to 8 inches, add sections of 5, 6, and/or 7X and still have a leader of twelve feet or so in length.

Incidentally, many novice anglers often hesitate to use the longer leaders, say those of twelve feet, as they are afraid they won't be able to make them turn over properly. This is a groundless fear, however. If the leader is properly designed, as are those in the table, even a twelve-footer will perform beautifully.

The above dry fly leaders function quite well under many circumstances. However, for much of my dry fly fishing, particularly under the most demanding conditions, I prefer a special leader developed by George Harvey. The "Harvey Leader" is designed roughly according to the 60/20/20 formula. However, it begins with a much lighter butt section, and it uses hard (stiff) nylon for the butt two thirds and soft (limp) nylon for the tip one third. It is designed not to straighten out, but to lie down in a series of gentle slack line waves to reduce potential drag on the fly. As George says, "It doesn't make sense to cast a slack line, if your leader is going to be straight."

George takes great pains to fine tune his tippet length with every change of flies. He'll tie on a fly and cast just the leader and a short length of line to observe how the leader falls to the water. If it fails to land in the proper waves, he'll shorten or lengthen the tippet as necessary. The slight amount of extra time and effort required for this fine tuning pays off handsomely in more effective presentations and more fish.

The specifications for a "Harvey Leader" are shown in the accompanying table.

Leader lengths for streamers, wet flies and nymphs are another matter, and it is here that you will find a greater range of theories among experienced fly fishermen. My own philosophy goes something like this. If I am fishing a fairly shallow stream and am using a floating line with sunken flies, I use my standard dry fly leader as described above. In such cases, I may add a small bit of lead above the first leader knot, tie a section of lead core line into the leader, or use weighted flies to help sink them to the proper depth.

When I am required to switch to a sinking or sinking-tip line in order to sink the fly more deeply in either a lake or a river, I generally shorten my leader considerably. With modern fast sinking lines, the line itself may sink quickly to the desired depth, but if the leader is too long, the fly will tend to ride a good deal higher in the water. By shortening the leader to three feet or less, the fly can be made to ride at the depth of the line.

Today my standard "wet" leader consists of merely a heavy butt section (.019 to .021 inch in diameter) about twelve inches long with a loop tied in the end. To this butt I then join a tippet of the appropriate diameter and about two feet in length. Under most conditions, such a leader performs admirably, and I have not been able to discern any adverse effect of having the leader so short.

Occasionally, though, conditions will cause me to modify my short leader. If, for example, I'm fishing over heavy weeds, the fly might sink too deeply and constantly become fouled. In that case, I switch to a standard leader of 7½ to 9 feet in length. Then, though the line may sink into the weeds, the fly tends to ride a little higher and will miss most of the weeds. Also, if fishing very clear water for difficult fish, I may stretch the sinking leader out to twelve feet or even longer.

Perhaps the most important rule of thumb for sinking leaders is to experiment, find out what works the best for you under most conditions, and then be willing to change as conditions dictate.

In summary, the proper leader is a very important link in the fly fishing system, and care should be taken to insure that it is functioning properly. If your leader fails to perform as it should, check the following points; they are all mistakes commonly made by novice fly fishers.

Is the leader too light in the butt section? If so, it will tend to land in a tangled heap on the water rather than turn over as it should. An improper taper can cause the same problem. When using the Harvey Leader with its light butt, this should not occur if a slight amount of extra "punch" is given to the cast.

Does the leader seem to turn over well except for the last couple of feet? It could be that the tippet is too long or too light for the particular fly being used.

Does the knot often come loose at the fly? Perhaps the tippet is too small in diameter for the fly being used. Or does the leader break at one of the other knots? Check your knot tying technique and be sure that you have a difference of no more than .002 inch between adjacent leader sections.

Do fish seem to approach your fly as if they are about to take it, but then turn and reject it at the last instant? If so, the tippet diameter may be so large that it either frightens the fish or causes unnatural drag on the fly—try a finer tippet.

The leader is probably the least expensive piece of tackle that you own, but its true value cannot be measured in dollars and cents. If you give a little thought and attention to detail in its construction, it will perform its many tasks admirably and will help you to consistently catch more fish. And that's the thing fishing reputations are built upon.

4X GEORGE HARVEY STYLE LEADER

Diameter		Length
.017 inch		10 inches
.015 inch	hard	20 inches
.013 inch	nylon	20 inches
.011 inch	_____	20 inches
.009 inch	soft	12 inches
.008 inch	nylon	18 inches
.007 inch	_____	22-28 inches

5X GEORGE HARVEY STYLE LEADER

Diameter		Length
.017 inch		10 inches
.015 inch	hard	20 inches
.013 inch	nylon	20 inches
.011 inch		20 inches
.009 inch	_____	12 inches
.008 inch	soft	12 inches
.007 inch	nylon	18 inches
.006 inch	_____	22-30 inches

LEADER SPECIFICATIONS
COURTESY OF THE ORVIS CO.

7½ Foot Leaders

0X	1X	2X	3X	4X
24" - .019"	24" - .019"	24" - .019"	24" - .019"	24" - .019"
16" - .017"	16" - .017"	16" - .017"	16" - .017"	16" - .017"
14" - .015"	14" - .015"	14" - .015"	14" - .015"	14" - .015"
9" - .013"	9" - .013"	9" - .013"	6" - .013"	6" - .013"
9" - .012"	9" - .011"	9" - .011"	6" - .011"	6" - .011"
18" - .011"	18" - .010"	18" - .009"	6" - .009"	6" - .009"
			18" - .008"	18" - .007"

9 Foot Leaders

0X	1X	2X	3X	4X	5X*
36" - .021"	36" - .021"	36" - .021"	36" - .021"	36" - .021"	36" - .021"
16" - .019"	16" - .019"	16" - .019"	16" - .019"	16" - .019"	14" - .019"
12" - .017"	12" - .017"	12" - .017"	12" - .017"	12" - .017"	12" - .017"
8" - .015"	8" - .015"	8" - .015"	6" - .015"	6" - .015"	10" - .015"
8" - .013"	8" - .013"	8" - .013"	6" - .013"	6" - .013"	6" - .013"
8" - .012"	8" - .012"	8" - .011"	6" - .011"	6" - .011"	6" - .011"
20" - .011"	20" - .010"	20" - .009"	6" - .009"	6" - .009"	6" - .009"
			20" - .008"	20" - .007"	6" - .007"
					20" - .006"

12 Foot Leaders

4X	5X	6X	7X*
36" - .021"	36" - .021"	36" - .021"	28" - .021"
24" - .019"	24" - .019"	24" - .019"	18" - .019"
16" - .017"	16" - .017"	16" - .017"	16" - .017"
12" - .015"	12" - .015"	12" - .015"	14" - .015"
7" - .013"	7" - .013"	7" - .013"	12" - .013"
7" - .011"	7" - .011"	7" - .011"	7" - .011"
7" - .009"	7" - .009"	7" - .009"	7" - .009"
7" - .008"	7" - .008"	7" - .007"	7" - .007"
28" - .007"	28" - .006"	28" - .005"	7" - .005"
			28" - .004"

*NOTE: The 9' - 5X and the 12' - 7X leaders are the author's tapers.

28.

Fisherman's Fall

F ly fishing seems to have been analyzed almost to death, and virtually every aspect of the sport has been minutely scrutinized. We have scientifically investigated fly rod construction and actions, fly floatant formulae, and leader materials. We have studied limnology, ecology, psychology and entomology. We have pursued the breeding of chickens, the development of plastics, the creation of exotic space age materials, and the proper means for handling road killed animals. We have inspected the genitalia of prepubescent insects.

Yet, despite all of this incredible scholarly activity, one area of the serious angler's life remains untouched by profound research. No instruction manuals are available from manufacturers of fishing tackle, and the subject is given only a fleeting mention — if it is considered at all, in most fly fishing schools.

I refer, of course, to the fisherman's fall. Apparently, the only major reference in the literature to the fisherman's fall is an obscure book of that name written by a Canadian fellow with a hyphenated name. Someday I hope to read it. In the meantime, I feel that it is my duty, in a book of this nature, to shed as much light as possible upon this much neglected aspect of our beloved sport.

It is odd that the fisherman's fall has been given so little attention in angling literature, since it is an experience every angler has shared. The angler who says that he or she has never fallen into the water is either a compulsive prevaricator or hasn't fished very much — or both.

It often occurs something like this. On a day when the sky is blue and the air crisp, you stand hip deep in a sparkling stream. Time stands still, birds sing, the cool water presses against your rubber clad legs; and you, the rod, the line, the fly and the river are as one. You, the angler, are as much a part of the environment as a streamside rock or a predatory shore bird. It is a good feeling, and one that I have found nowhere but with a fly rod in my hand.

Sometimes, though, our oneness with the environment is carried literally one step too far. It is that instant when time again becomes a conscious reality, but its passage seems to occur in slow motion.

All who fly fish know that moment. The current is suddenly too strong and the water too deep. The sand beneath our felt-soled feet is washed away, and we flail our arms madly to retain our equilibrium as we dance downstream on tip-toe. Then there is no bottom at all. The cold water engulfs us with a wild rush, and our oneness with the environment is complete.

I began my serious research into this phenomenon at an early age. In fact, I have been known as an intrepid wader since boyhood. This undoubtedly came about from the fact that the river Trepid passed but a short distance from my home and was my favorite fishing spot. I would fall into the stream with some regularity, and when I did, one of my fun-loving fishing companions would always shout, "Hey, Dave's in Trepid again!"

After many years of in-depth study of the subject, I have developed a catalog of fine and fancy fishermen's falls, that I would now like to offer to the general fishing public. Of course, I am not speaking of the routine little trips, stumbles, and generally klutz-like behavior that is all too common in everyday angling. I am speaking only of the great ones. The ones that combine style, grace and originality with a flair for showmanship. The Oscar-winning performances, as it were.

Each particular example will be named and described as I originally performed it. Readers should feel free, however, to embellish the original in any manner they see fit. After all, extra points can be scored for originality and creativity, as I have mentioned. Let my work be merely a beginning, and may it stimulate you to your own efforts.

Incidentally, the scoring system generally used here in northern Idaho is the Pat McManus Patented Scoring System. For those interested in the competitive aspect of the fisherman's fall, I refer you to Pat's work on the subject.[1] I generally feel little need to compete, but simply participate for the pure joy of the experience.

Let us begin.

The Slide

The Slide was my first great one. It was the one that stimulated me to begin a career of lifelong research on the topic.

The Slide was developed during the first season of my trout fishing life while I was living in Minnesota on the north shore of Lake Superior. In pursuit of steelhead, I had walked down a wooded path that was covered with Minnesota's first light snowfall of the year, and was headed toward the "slides" on the Stewart River. The sun had just risen, and the morning was cold, white and beautiful.

The slides is aptly named. It is a spot that seemed to have wanted to become a waterfall, but didn't quite make it. Instead, the water rushes over a rock ledge at an angle of about thirty degrees. It boils and foams

[1]McManus, Pat, "How to Go Splat!", *The Grasshopper Trap*, Holt, Rinehart and Winston, N.Y., 1985.

and roars for some thirty yards before dropping three feet or so into the round, placid, deep pool which I intended to fish. On either side, the slides is flanked by sheer rock cliffs.

An angler with plenty of time can hike around the slides to the waiting pool, but in the fall, when the water is low, one can carefully walk down the rock ledge close to the rampant water and safely reach the pool. That was my intent.

Unfortunately, I hadn't considered the light snowfall, and I had not expected the thin coating of ice that covered every rock within reach of the heavy spray from the boiling river. I started over the crest of the slides, and almost immediately began a slide of my own. At first I stood like a skier shushing down a torrent of water, then with a graceful half twist, I fell to my knees and continued in the full reverse position. This, of course, would have been worth additional style points under the McManus System.

Halfway down, I completed my maneuver with another half twist, and found myself lying flat on my back. As I completed the roll, I caught a quick glimpse of another angler beside the waiting pool. Fearing that I would sink into the depths of the pool, I continued to roll sideways toward the edge of the slides. That resulted in both good news and bad news.

The good news was that I rolled out of the slides and hung up on a rock outcrop just at the very brink of the three foot drop into the pool. The bad news was that I was on the wrong side of the river.

As I sheepishly looked up to find the other angler, I discovered that he was bending over to lift out a large steelhead. After admiring his catch, he turned and walked off down the stream. He never saw me.

My walk down the river, back up around the slides, and through the snow covered woods remains vividly etched in my memory. How wonderful it is to be out in the northern woods after the first snowfall of the year.

The Magnificent Mud Flop

Water does not have to be either deep or fast to provide an excellent opportunity for creative falling. The Magnificent Mud Flop offers a classic example.

John Randolph and I were preparing to fish O'Dell's Spring Creek in Montana and had walked across a meadow to gain access to the stream. Nearing the river we came to a wide, shallow puddle left by an earlier rainfall. John started to walk around the puddle, which seemed ridiculous, since we were wearing waders and were about to go walking in a river, so I started into the water. It appeared to be no more than three or four inches deep.

"It looks kind of muddy," John said as he stood his ground.

"Oh, it'll be O.K.," I replied. "No sweat."

I was right—almost. The water was only about four inches deep.

The mud, on the other hand, after about five steps into it, came to above my knees.

I struggled to cross, but finally, as I was tugging to pull out for another step, my foot slipped up into the wader. The wader foot remained firmly imbedded in mud. Since I had been leaning forward attempting to pull out of the mud and walk, I had plenty of inertia to complete my chosen maneuver—the Magnificent Mud Flop.

Knowing the importance of the proper form in order to achieve the full point value of the stunt, I flung my arms wide, while retaining a firm grip on my fly rod. (I prefer the thumb on top grip, by the way.) My spread-eagled body made a perfectly flat landing, and the resulting *splat!* was timed precisely to compliment my joyous shout.

Perfection is difficult to achieve, but is well worth the extra effort.

The Great Guide's Gaffe

No one is quite as inspiring of utter confidence as an Alaskan guide. He can face any situation with aplomb. Neither grizzly bear nor miles of untracked wilderness hold any threat for these staunch protectors, friends and leaders of the angler.

Though not completely without a sense of humor, many Alaskan guides take a dim view of the foibles of the common angler. An Alaskan guide is far from ordinary. Thus, I was delighted when the opportunity arose for me to develop a particularly outstanding example of my unique talent especially for these dedicated, hardworking men of the North—the Great Guide's Gaffe.

I had spent a week as a guest at the Bristol Bay Lodge in the Wood River-Tikchik Lake region of Alaska, and shortly before the end of my stay, a family emergency called one of the regular guides away. The lodge manager, who had a large group coming in the following week, asked me if I would consider staying an extra week to help with the guiding. That was like asking a kid if he'd like an ice cream cone, and I immediately agreed to do it.

I moved into the guide's quarters and immediately felt six inches taller. While shaving the next morning, I noticed that my eyes had taken on a steely glint and a not unattractive squint that I hadn't noticed before. I think it must have been the northern air or something.

I met my first group of clients and tried to maintain the casual air of elegance that I had witnessed in the other guides, and I seemed to pull it all off quite well. I answered questions with authority, gave advice on tackle, and assured the clients that they were in for a real experience on this, their first trip to Alaska. They seemed impressed.

After a short flight to the Agulapak River, our float plane scraped to a stop on the sandy beach, and the pilot jumped out to secure us. I stepped out onto the pontoon to assist the others in leaving the plane, and since there wasn't much room on the float, I decided to step off into the shallow water. It looked to be about two feet deep.

It was my good fortune that the water was actually two feet and six inches deep — a fact that permitted me to develop the Great Guide's Gaffe on the spot and with very little forethought. The slight extra depth to the clear water, as I stepped into it with my left foot, allowed my right foot to hang up on the plane's float and to remain there while I performed a graceful clockwise half twist. The twist completed, I landed flat on my back at the feet of my first day's clients.

I felt that it was important for them to realize that even Alaskan guides have a sense of humor.

The Full Twist With A Full Reverse

Sometimes a perfectly average fall can be completed in a manner that immediately more than doubles its scoring potential, or at the very least, makes it considerably more enjoyable if you don't happen to be going for points. The Full Twist With A Full Reverse is just such a stunt, although I must say in advance that it requires an ideal set of circumstances to pull it off.

John Merwin and I were on a photography expedition to the Madison River in Yellowstone Park. John was then the editor of *Fly Fisherman* and we were shooting a variety of photos for possible use in the magazine. I had been doing the posing and John the photography. In fact, you may have seen one of our shots. The photo of the guy standing in the water casting a nice loop that is used in one of *FFM's* subscription brochures is me, and it was taken that day.

John spotted a nice trout feeding regularly just upstream from where we had been shooting, and he suggested that it would be a great idea if I could get into position to cast to the fish. He also said that he'd appreciate it if I would catch it. Editors like to suggest things like that.

I slipped out of the river and moved upstream to be in a better casting position for the rising fish. Those of you who have fished the Madison in the Park undoubtedly know that its bottom is covered with grassy hummocks and bumps of all sorts. It was this natural stream configuration which led to my perfection of the Full Twist With A Full Reverse.

My complete attention was on the feeding fish, and as I stepped into the river, my foot inadvertently landed upon one of the grassy hummocks. When I placed my weight on it, the foot slipped off the hummock, wedged securely between it and the bank, and held me tightly. The result was the full twist and an immediate *splash!* as I fell face first into the river.

That was the easy part and was perfectly ordinary up to that point. The clincher was the full reverse, which came after I rolled over to a back floating position and started to laugh uncontrollably.

"What's the matter with you?" John demanded.

"I'm wearing your clothes!" I yelled between belly laughs.

Since we had been shooting so many pictures, I had worn several different outfits, so it would not look like the same angler in every photo. As a last resort, I had put on John's shirt, hat and fully loaded fishing vest.

John didn't seem to appreciate the significance of my newly developed maneuver, and his comments while he was removing everything from his vest to dry in the sun probably are of little importance to this discussion. It does prove once again, though, that editors are apparently totally lacking in humor.

The Double Dip

Steelheading in the West provides an abundance of opportunities to develop a personal repertoire of fisherman's falls. It is also one of the most common locations to perfect the various "doubles." The easiest for the novice will be the simple Double Dip.

I did my first Double Dip on Idaho's Clearwater River not far from my home in Moscow. The late Gary Crawford, an outdoor writer from Minnesota, was a friend of mine, and he wanted to write a steelhead story. At that time, the locals didn't want any publicity for the river, and I wanted to keep my friends, so I offered to guide him, if he wouldn't name the river. He agreed.

One of the first rules that I learned as a steelheader is always carry an extra set of clothing. The water is heavy and cold, and the rocks are slippery, and it's no fun driving home soaking wet.

True to form, after fishing for an hour or so I slipped on a rock and took a silly, everyday fall. Undaunted, I went back to the car, changed into my dry clothes and hung the wet ones on the car in a futile attempt to dry them in the cold autumn air. Since we didn't have the making of a story at that point, I slipped on a spare pair of waders and went back into the river to fish.

After fishing for another thirty minutes or so, I heard a shout from somewhere downstream, and looked up just in time to see Gary's wife, Jan, sink from view into the heavy water. I was about to yell something wise to her as she surfaced, but the distraction was my undoing — another step, another slippery rock, and down I went again to complete my Double Dip.

Gary did get his story, and I was delighted to find the history of my Double Dip fully documented. One is rarely so fortunate. When a copy of Gary's magazine arrived, I found that the one photo of his trip that had been published was one of me naked with only a towel wrapped around my waist and my cowboy hat on my head. In the background, my two sets of clothes were spread all over the car, and my underwear waved gallantly from the antenna.

The Lobby Lunge

While this manuscript was being written, it became quite clear that a break from my work routine was in order, and that a field research trip was absolutely necessary. Thus, I did the only logical thing, and booked a fishing trip to the Bow River. Little did I realize that the trip would not only provide an incredible opportunity for me to express my creativity, but would likely place me solidly into the records books for years to come.

The clients of Streamside Guide Service in Calgary are normally booked into the Atrium of the Hospitality Inn, which provides excellent accommodations. The Atrium features a very large lobby filled with narrow pathways through abundant vegetation, sparkling fountains and reflecting pools flush with the floor, a Jacuzzi and the main swimming pool. In short, it's a very attractive place.

Thoughts of greatness were the farthest thing from my mind as I entered the lobby of the Atrium late on my first evening. But, as they say, greatness finds those who are deserving, and when opportunity knocks, the door must be opened.

Completely engrossed in my conversation with Jim Sawhill, my fishing partner, I headed down one of the dimly lit pathways through the fountains. The path turned. I didn't. Thus, with one magnificent step, I became the first angler in history to fall in while in the hotel lobby the night *before* going fishing.

The Really Stupid Double Slide

This chapter began with a discussion of The Slide, and it is only appropriate to end it with an advanced variation—the Really Stupid Double Slide. If you feel that you have not progressed to the level necessary for this stunt, you may want to just glance over it for now. You can study it in more detail when you feel ready for it.

Frankly, the execution of the Really Stupid Double Slide is quite easy, and when performed by an expert, it appears to be the utmost in simplicity. Do not be deceived! Remember that an expert can make anything look easy—that's why he's the expert. To have any chance of success with the Really Stupid Double Slide, you have to be really stupid.

I qualified for the honor in Pennsylvania in 1968. I had spent the entire summer on a high altitude research project in the Colorado mountains and had fished several times a week in husky mountain streams without once shipping a drop of water. Back in Pennsylvania, I decided to end the trout season on placid little Big Fishing Creek. That decision was my undoing.

Late in the afternoon on the final day of the season, I found myself walking along the river's edge in dark shadows. It had been a good day, and I was feeling very mellow. I wasn't paying much attention to where I was walking.

Then the fatal step. I placed my foot down heavily on a large, flat, slippery piece of shale and immediately slipped slowly into the stream. My hat drifted off down the river.

The following spring, I decided to open the new trout season on Big

Fishing Creek. It is important to note here that at the time, I had no thought of achieving the Really Stupid Double Slide. I was merely going fishing.

But fame and good fortune seem to have a way of finding worthy candidates at the most unlikely times, and the opening of the trout season was to be my day. I hadn't fished for thirty minutes when I located *the same large, flat, slippery piece of shale* that I had stepped on to end the previous season, *and I stepped on it again!* The result was remarkably similar to the first occasion.

Now that's really stupid.

29.

"He Was a
Strange Old Man"

The gnarled fingers eased their pressure on the smooth cork. Blue veins on the back of his hand stood out like so many rivers flowing sluggishly beneath the thin, dry skin. His vision was cloudy, and he was no longer aware of the sterile surroundings or the pretty lady in white who sat nearby.

But he could still feel the silken cork, polished smooth by untold thousands of casts. His fingers slid over the graceful curve of the grip, and hesitated slightly before coming to rest on the six-sided sliver of cane that quivered at his touch.

He had been a young man when he built the rod; young and strong like the cane he had split to build it. It was still a good rod, he thought to himself. Only he had aged.

He could remember it as though it were yesterday. The long hours of planing, measuring, filing and sanding to get exactly the right taper. He remembered the sudden sting as a careless move had caused the razor-like edge of the bamboo to bite into his hand and how his first thought had been to wipe the blood from the strip before it left a stain. He had tapered the thin strips of cane until they were accurate to a thousandth of an inch, and almost cried when he jammed one into the end of his workbench and it shattered into a hundred splinters.

Finally, when the strips were perfect, he had glued them together and fitted them with the finest German silver ferrule. Using his fingers rather than trusting a brush, he had applied several thin coats of varnish to the stick and polished it with pumice and water. The guides had been wrapped with fine silk thread, varnished, and at last the rod was completed.

He hadn't been able to wait for spring, but fitted a fine English reel to the seat and went out into the cold winter air to make his first casts. He had stood knee-deep in the snow, his hands shaking as he threaded the line through the guides for the first time. With a practiced rhythm he had started false casting and extended line until he had forty feet of the double taper singing back and forth in narrow loops. He had smiled as he released the coils from his left hand, shot another fifteen feet of loose line, and watched it settle softly to the snow. It was good.

Spring had been a long time coming that year; he had thought it might never come, as he sat night after night at his vise tying flies for the approaching season. He had built the rod for one reason — to fish his beloved little Kispi. Then he had begun to fill his fly boxes for the same reason. Each evening a dozen size 18 black beetles or fur ants would come from his vise — or midge pupae, or exquisite size 20 or 24 blue duns, or cream, or badger, or olive dry flies. The Kispi was that kind of a stream.

Each evening, before going to bed, he had taken the new rod from its pegs on the wall just to admire his handiwork and to feel the smooth cork in his hand and the resilient spring in the slender strips of cane. Seven feet long and a hair over two ounces, it would cast the lightest fly line. It was perfect.

The first warm weekend in March had found him hiking on snowshoes along his little stream. The banks still were covered with deep snow, but the bubbling springs had kept the stream itself free of ice and he had been able to watch the cruising trout as he sat in the sun and ate a cold sandwich. As he had filled his pipe, a good fish had risen to pluck a drifting midge pupa from just beneath the smooth surface of the water. He had heard the audible *smack* as the pupa disappeared in a swirl, and he had watched the perfect circle of the rise until it dissolved in the slivers of ice that rimmed the bank. The first rise of the year, and the season was still two months away.

He had been a professor at a small Midwestern college when he had built the rod, and that year, as the leaden winter skies gave way to the bright blue of spring and the birds began to sing outside his window, it had seemed that the professor had a more acute case of spring fever than his students. The warm breeze was heavy with the sensual perfume of the lilac, and often it had required supreme concentration to keep his mind upon anatomy and physiology rather than allow it to drift off to the Kispi where the trout were sure to be rising to the earliest of the *Chironomidae*.

He had taken many long walks along the little stream that spring. By the time the last drift of snow had joined the placid spring-fed waters of the creek, he had mentally cataloged the hiding places of a half dozen out-sized brown trout. He had watched the fish cruise the perimeters of their pools and roll lazily on their sides to pick up drifting nymphs. He had seen them rise to midge pupae awash in the surface film, and had carefully observed their headlong dashes to the security of a half-submerged log or the cover of a rock when they had been frightened by the shadow of a bird or his own careless movement.

In his mind, he had caught each of "his" fish dozens of times as he plotted and planned just how he would approach each pool when the season finally opened. He had known what fly he would use and exactly where he would have to stand to cast. He had known where he would have to throw a slack line to avoid dragging the fly and where he would have to shoot a tight loop under an overhanging branch in order to present the fly to the largest of the fish. He had reviewed and rehearsed all these things a thousand times.

A low, involuntary moan escaped from his dry lips, and the lady in white looked up from her book as the old man shifted his position in the bed. She wondered why the faint smile crossed his lips as he moved the slim piece of cane through the air. Funny how he wouldn't let go of that thing, she thought.

The old man turned the handle of the small English reel that was still fitted to the delicate rod. He heard the beautiful music it produced, and, again, the faint smile passed across his thin, bluish lips. He was no longer aware of the dull pain that throbbed within his body.

The opening day of the trout season had finally come to the Kispi. In spite of his excitement, he had eaten a leisurely breakfast that day, and, after a second cup of steaming black coffee, had carefully slipped the rod into its new cloth bag and metal case. His tackle bag, flies, and waders had been inspected and packed the evening before, and he knew that he was ready.

He had not been surprised to find two cars parked beside the stream when he arrived. They were as familiar to him as his own and belonged to the other "Kispi regulars." He could have fished with them as was his custom, but that day he had chosen to go alone. He had known there would not be the opening day crush of anglers that was typical of most small streams in that area. The upper Kispi was special. The upper reaches of the little stream were not stocked by the state, and few realized that this part of the stream served as spawning water for a fine population of brook and brown trout. He knew that lunker browns of up to eight pounds had been taken from this water, and he had seen brookies that would have exceeded two pounds. Such fish were rare, of course, but it was enough to know that they were there.

Of the few who knew of the water, fewer yet fished it. He had fished many of the fabled streams of the country and knew that the Kispi was the most challenging of them all. The water, even on that opening day, had been low and clear and the fish as wary as they would be all season. This was not water for the bait fisherman or the casual fly fisherman. A gob of worms falling upon the water would send every fish in the pool darting for cover, and the careless fly fisherman would go fishless as well.

To the regulars, one fish from the upper Kispi was worth ten from any other river. It was enough to be on a stream where the water could be seen bubbling from underground springs and ran a constant forty-nine to fifty-two degrees even through the heat of the summer; a stream that offered solitude, and the opportunnity to catch stream-bred trout. The fish were deep-bellied, with the rich dark coloration not found in their hatchery cousins. Their meat was a deep orange with the delicate flavor that was missing in fish that had been hand-fed a diet of pellets.

The fish from the upper Kispi did not come easily. If a man were lucky, he might take several fish in a day, or he might take none at all even though they were rising all around him. The character of the fish and the water demanded perfection from the fisherman. Perfection was not often achieved, but it was enough just to be there.

Thus he had found himself, once again, preparing to begin a new season on the Kispi. With much care he had removed the new rod from its case and firmly fitted the silver ferrule together. The light Hardy reel was seated under the narrow silver bands, and the light line threaded through the fine snake guides. He had not hurried, but had savored every operation, like a gourmet rolling a mouthful of red wine across his tongue. The season would be long, and while he had thought it might never come, now that it had arrived there was no need to hurry.

When, at last, he had outfitted himself, he knotted a tiny size 18 *Chironomid* pupa to his finely tapered leader and walked slowly through the trees toward the stream. He had not begun to fish immediately, but had crossed the narrow stream just above the old iron bridge and paused to look at the Fence Pool. He had seen only one small brookie lying in the shadow of a patch of watercress, and no fish were actively feeding. The situation had been the same at the Pool-Above-the-Fence-Pool.

As he neared Big Red's Pool he had crouched on his knees in order to avoid throwing his shadow on the water, but try as he might, he could not spot the large, crimson-sided fish that had given the pool its name. He knew the fish would be lying beneath the scum patch at the narrow head of the pool, and had hoped that the trout would be feeding. He had seen the fish on many occasions and knew that it would weigh more than three pounds. It would have made a worthy adversary upon which to try the new rod. But it was not to be, so he had risen to his feet and walked on to Observation Pool.

The pool names, like the stream itself, were known mainly by the Kispi regulars. It had been the regulars who had been responsible for the names, and it gave them a means of discussing the stream and of describing their successes — or, more often, their failures. The pools had been named after distinguishing features, individuals or events, and the mention of any single name would call forth a dozen tales on any winter night when the regulars would gather around the fire to tie flies and swap yarns.

Observation Pool had been named for the small clump of willows which provided cover and allowed the fisherman to stand unseen to observe the fish in the pool.

The old man's hand tightened on the grip of the slender rod as he remembered what he had seen on that morning as he approached Observation Pool. He squeezed the rod until his knuckles were white, and again he could see in his mind the spreading rings on the water that signaled a good trout actively feeding.

The fish had been lying beneath a log jutting out from the bank. At regular intervals it would rise to some unseen insect drifting along the ridge of water that curled down the leading edge of the log. He had seen this fish several times during his pre-season trips to the river, and he knew that it was a solid brown trout of at least two pounds. He had watched patiently as the fish rose six, eight, a dozen times or more before he had slipped carefully into the still water and waded into casting position. He had never taken his eyes from the fish, and had breathed a sigh of relief each time the fish came up. He knew that it had not been frightened.

He had but a scant six feet to wade when the fish made its last rise. He had stood perfectly still in the water for more than fifteen minutes waiting for another rise that never came. He had spooked a smaller fish which he had not seen, and, in its flight for cover, the smaller fish had frightened the larger one. The Kispi was unforgiving of mistakes like that.

Somewhat dejectedly he had left the water, paused to fill his pipe, and walked up the stream. He had skipped several pools which he knew would be unproductive, and had crossed over to the Spring Hole. He saw no rising fish in the pool, so stopped only long enough for a drink of the cool, sweet water.

What he would give for a taste of the "Kispi champagne" now! Again, a groan slipped from his crusted lips, and the lady in white put down her book and walked out of the darkened room. He did not see her leave, but saw instead the boiling white sand where the Kispi bubbled from the ground. The water was so clear that flies on its surface seemed suspended in space over the moss and sand of the stream bed. He could feel the cold water drip from his nose as it had after so many long, cool drinks from the stream, and he remembered feeling the icy trickle that would always run down under his collar after he had risen to his feet. He shivered in his bed.

On that day, he had left the Spring Hole and walked to the Island Pool where a few small brookies had been taking midge pupae, but, seeking a big brown, he had gone on to the Lower and Middle Bridge Pools. Again, except for a few smaller fish, all had been quiet. In the Middle Bridge Pool he had spotted one brownie of perhaps fifteen inches lying just on the edge of a bed of moss, but the fish had not been feeding and, after watching it for a few minutes, he had continued on to the Upper Bridge Pool.

The pool had been quiet when he reached the abutment of the upper bridge. He had sat on a rock, relit his pipe, and was watching a cedar waxwing pluck insects from the air when he heard the *smack* that indicated the rise of a good fish. Before the rings had completely disappeared from the water, the fish rose again near the head of the pool. Five times he had watched the fish rise before he had taken the fly from the hook keeper on his rod. He greased the leader to within an inch of the fly, and he knew the tiny artificial would drift just under the surface of the water like the naturals that the fish was taking each time it rose.

The fish was a long way off, but this time he had taken no chances of putting it down by wading. He had stood on the rock where he had been sitting and began to extend his line by false casting. He was far enough from the fish so that even when he was standing he could not be seen. He had kept his backcast low to put it under the bridge, and when the little piece of cane was straining to cast all the line it could support, he had shot an extra ten or twelve feet of line and prayed it would be enough.

He had held his breath as the fly settled gently to the water about three feet upstream from the fish and a couple of feet to one side. Then he had watched as the leader point drifted downstream, untouched.

Just as he was certain that he had put the fish down with his cast, the big trout rose again, and once more he had dropped his fly above the feeding fish. Three times the scene had been repeated, and each time his fly had been refused.

He had not dared to cast directly over the fish for fear of putting it down, and the distance had been too great to accurately throw a curve into the leader. But, just as he released the line on his fourth cast, a gentle puff of wind pushed the little fly a foot from its intended target and nearer to the feeding fish. Again the fish rose, and this time he had lifted his rod to feel the solid weight that told him the fly had done its job.

Instantly a huge boil appeared in the water and the little Hardy began to sing. He had dropped his rod a bit to remove some of the pressure from the fragile leader, and the trout, not wanting to cross the shallow riffle into the next pool, began to circle back toward him. He had frantically stripped in line, but had been unable to match the speed of the frightened fish. He had been amazed to find the fish still hooked when he managed to tighten the line once more.

Feeling the renewed tension, the trout again headed for the top of the pool. He could still remember the hum of the line as it cut through the water, and again he felt the fear he had felt when he expected the huge fish to reach the cover of the brush pile where it would surely have been lost. The slender piece of cane bent and took the full pressure of the fish, and he had been able to feel the fish's power down into his wrist. This would indeed be a test of his workmanship. Would the slivers of cane stand the strain? Would the glue hold? Had he taken off too much wood at the ferrule? A hundred questions had flown through his mind, and even now, in his bed, the muscles of his stomach tightened as he again played the fish in his mind.

Once more the fish had turned and headed back toward him, and once more he had been forced to recover line as rapidly as he could. This time, however, the fish had not returned as quickly and he had been able to maintain tension on the line. The fish settled to the bottom, and he had been able to feel the big head as it shook from side to side in a futile attempt to free itself from the sting of the small hook.

Through it all the little rod had taken the strain and bent like a sapling in the wind, springing this way and that as the great fish fought for its life. Always the wand bent to absorb the shock of a sudden rush, and always it kept the nagging pressure upon the trout.

How long the fight had continued he did not know, but gradually he had come to realize that he was the master of the situation. The fish's struggles had slowly lost their power and its runs were neither as long nor as swift. Finally, he had lowered his rod and let the exhausted fish slip back into the bag of his waiting net. The rod had lost its virginity.

He had gently removed the tiny fly from the mouth of the fish, and he let it lie for a moment in the net. It had been a huge, hook-jawed old male, and he could still picture the golden yellow of its broad side. It had looked like burnished brass flecked with black, and the belly had darkened to a mottled gray. He had, for a brief instant, imagined the fish hanging over the fireplace in his den, but immediately had known that he could do no such thing. He had won and his rod had held. He could ask no more. Carefully he removed the fish from the net, held it into the current, and gently moved it back and forth to pump life-giving oxygen back into its gills. At last the fish had grown strong in his hands, and he opened them. With a sweep of its broad tail, the fish had disappeared.

The slender rod had proven itself many times since that day so long ago. There had been other rods and many streams, but always the little Kispi rod had been his favorite. It had taken fat brook trout from remote ponds in Maine, grayling and cutthroat from high mountain streams in Montana, brown trout from the limestone waters of Pennsylvania and leaping rainbows from the Pacific Northwest. Always it had been equal to the tasks he had given it. Now, except for a few more coats of varnish and a new set of guides, the rod was exactly as it had been the day he finished building it. The corks showed the soft patina of age, but the cane itself was as straight and resilient as it had always been.

Now the old man was once again on the Upper Bridge Pool of the Kispi, and again he saw the dimple and heard the smack of a giant brown trout taking midge pupae from the surface film. Once again he was standing on a rock, extending his line toward the fish and praying that his little rod would stand the strain. He could not feel the hands that touched his fevered body or hear the voices slowly counting and reciting numbers to unseen ears. There was only the Kispi, the fish, and his little rod. The fish rolled one more time, and then there was nothing.

The man in the green coat removed the stethoscope from his ears and spoke to the pretty lady in white. "He was a strange old man, wasn't he?"

"Yes, he was. He sure didn't want to let go of that fish pole. It's sort of sad the way old folks become so attached to something so worthless. He had no family or friends that we know of; what will we do with the pole?"

"Well, it's just an old-fashioned wooden one, but I can.take it up to the lake. The kids will have fun catching bullheads with it off the dock." And he took the rod from the old man's still fingers for the last time.